TAIWAN STRAIT
DILEMMAS

Significant Issues Series

Timely books presenting current CSIS research and analysis of interest to the academic, business, government, and policy communities.
Managing editor: Roberta L. Howard

The **Center for Strategic and International Studies (CSIS)**, established in 1962, is a private, tax-exempt institution focusing on international public policy issues. Its research is nonpartisan and nonproprietary.

CSIS is dedicated to policy analysis and impact. It seeks to inform and shape selected policy decisions in government and the private sector to meet the increasingly complex and difficult global challenges that leaders will confront in this new century. It achieves this mission in four ways: by generating strategic analysis that is anticipatory and interdisciplinary; by convening policymakers and other influential parties to assess key issues; by building structures for policy action; and by developing leaders.

CSIS does not take specific public policy positions. Accordingly, all views, positions, and conclusions expressed in this publication should be understood to be solely those of the authors.

The CSIS Press
Center for Strategic and International Studies
1800 K Street, N.W., Washington, D.C. 20006
Telephone: (202) 887-0200   Fax: (202) 775-3199
E-mail: books@csis.org   Web site: http://www.csis.org/

TAIWAN STRAIT

DILEMMAS

CHINA–TAIWAN–U.S. POLICIES

IN THE NEW CENTURY

EDITED BY GERRIT W. GONG

Foreword by Richard C. Bush

THE CSIS PRESS

**Center for Strategic
and International Studies**
Washington, D.C.

Significant Issues Series, Volume 22, Number 1
© 2000 by the Center for Strategic and International Studies
Washington, D.C. 20006
Printed on recycled paper in the United States of America

04 03 02 01 00   5 4 3 2 1

ISSN 0736-7136
ISBN 0-89206-363-7

Library of Congress Cataloging-in-Publication Data
CIP information available upon request

Cover design by Robert L. Wiser, Archetype Press, Washington, D.C.

CONTENTS

FOREWORD

Richard C. Bush

ONE OF THE SALUTARY DEVELOPMENTS IN EAST ASIA in the early 1990s was the beginning of semiofficial interchange between the two sides of the Taiwan Strait. The most obvious example of this contact was the meeting between Koo Chen-fu and Wang Daohan in Singapore in March 1993. In addition, there was cooperation between the Straits Exchange Foundation and the Association for Relations Across the Taiwan Strait in solving practical problems and in facilitating a wide variety of exchanges. Beyond semiofficial encounters were expanding private contacts, particularly in the areas of trade and investment. All this fostered hope that the political dispute between Beijing and Taipei might be resolved amicably and over time, thus removing one of East Asia's most enduring flash points.

Obviously, such optimism was deflated when tensions increased after Taiwan president Lee Teng-hui's June 1995 visit to the United States and the PRC's high-profile military exercises in the latter half of 1995 and March 1996. After a long stalemate, dialogue resumed when Koo Chen-fu visited Shanghai and Beijing in October 1998. Wang Daohan was to make a return visit in the fall of 1999. In July 1999, however, President Lee announced that cross-strait ties were "a special state-to-state relationship." Tensions increased again and then declined in September. Other actions and reactions over the past five years have contributed to an atmosphere of mistrust and misunderstanding, which Taiwan's democratic system has made only more complicated.

At the heart of this stalemate is a set of substantive disagreements over issues like sovereignty, PRC use of force, Taiwan's international role, and where to focus cross-strait dialogue once it resumes. These are not easy issues. Resolving them will require both creativity and political will by Beijing and Taipei alone. The United States does not intend to insert itself. (Washington does have an abiding interest that any resolution be peaceful, and it understands the reality that any arrangements arrived at will have to be acceptable to the people on Taiwan.)

Given this impasse, it is fortunate that organizations like the Center for Strategic and International Studies have sponsored periodic dialogues between influential scholars from the PRC and Taiwan. These discussions, conducted outside the glare of publicity and unconstrained by the positions of the two governments, fill an important gap. They allow the individuals on one side to understand the perspective of the other, and the intensity with which it is held. They permit in-depth consideration of the substantive issues that divide the two sides. Scholars can also discuss ideas for bridging gaps in ways that officials cannot. Ultimately, of course, it is political leaders who will have to take the creative ideas of scholars and mobilize support for the realization of those ideas.

The papers in this volume were originally presented at a CSIS forum held in late 1999. They demonstrate both the difficulty of the substantive issues and the intellectual talent that exists on both sides of the strait. They provide a snapshot of the intricacies of the cross-strait problem at a critical time at a conceptual and practical level. Untying these knots remains a challenge, but dialogues such as this one increase the probability of doing so. The reason for doing so is clear and compelling: establishing an enduring peace in one of the world's most vital and important regions.

PREFACE

Gerrit W. Gong

FOUR ENDURING POLICY ISSUES that are key to peace, stability, and prosperity in the Taiwan Strait in the new century are presented here. They are the real issues, in real time, in the words, logic, and emotion of leading experts from the People's Republic of China (PRC), Taiwan, and the United States.

A first issue concerns frameworks and ambiguities.

The United States has built a policy framework for dealing with the PRC and Taiwan on three Sino-U.S. communiqués and the Taiwan Relations Act. The three communiqués are the February 1972 Shanghai Communiqué, the 1978 Joint Communiqué on the Establishment of Diplomatic Relations, and the August 17, 1982, Joint Communiqué. The U.S. Congress enacted the Taiwan Relations Act in 1979 to help maintain peace, security, and stability in the western Pacific and to continue commercial, cultural, and other relations between the people of the United States and the people on Taiwan.

These three Sino-U.S. communiqués and the Taiwan Relations Act provide a framework for dealing with the dynamic ambiguities that exist across the Taiwan Strait. In 1972, as the Shanghai communiqué states, one ambiguity was that all Chinese on either side of the Taiwan Strait maintain that there is but one China and that Taiwan is a part of China. Now, 28 years later in 2000, particularly Taiwan's democratization and a nascent native Taiwanese cultural identity (and possibly Taiwanese nationalism) fuel a growing debate in the United States and elsewhere.

One issue is whether the established "one-China" framework promulgated in the three communiqués and the Taiwan Relations Act is sufficient to maintain cross-strait peace, prosperity, and stability—or whether past frameworks and ambiguities must be redefined in the face of current and future challenges. Another issue is whether ambiguities inherent within, and integral to, the frameworks provided by these past agreements and understandings now contribute to cross-strait stability or instability.

The Clinton administration has sought to preserve both strategic clarity and tactical ambiguity regarding its obligations under the three communiqués and the Taiwan Relations Act to defend Taiwan in certain circumstances. Asserting unwavering U.S. commitment while maintaining flexibility to implement according to circumstance was a crux issue when the Clinton administration sent two U.S. aircraft carrier battle groups to the Taiwan Strait area after Beijing engaged in military and missile exercises there in 1995 and 1996.

Concerned that cross-strait ambiguities are inherently destabilizing and could, including by accident or miscalculation, involve U.S. forces in Taiwan Strait military confrontation, some in the United States and elsewhere have come to opposite conclusions. There are those who want to declare a specific U.S. intent to defend Taiwan; in contrast, others want to specify conditions (such as Taiwan's declaring independence) in which the United States would not defend Taiwan. Similarly, some argue for removing current ambiguities regarding Taiwan's international status by recognizing Taiwan as an independent country. Conversely, others argue for stating "one China" and its three-no's corollaries (no Taiwan independence; no one China, one Taiwan; no membership in international organizations requiring statehood) so unequivocally as to limit any separation of Taiwan from the mainland.

This kind of cross-strait tug and pull, including historical perceptions and memories, prompted a discussion in the United States of cross-strait frameworks and ambiguities, including the possible merits of interim modus vivendi. All this appears to have a time frame: It is the period from March 18, 2000, when Taiwan elects a new president, to November 2000 when the United States elects a new president, to fall 2002 when China's 16th party congress may select new Chinese leaders. Particularly during this potential crossroads period, new leaders and new administrations will consider whether new understandings, new arrangements, or new agreements are feasible or desirable regarding Taiwan Strait frameworks and policies.

Harry Harding, in his chapter herein, considers the possible role of interim arrangements in evolving Taiwan Strait frameworks. Harding begins with three assumptions: The current situation in the Taiwan Strait remains unstable; a final resolution of the Taiwan question is inconceivable in the short to medium term; therefore, some kind of interim arrangements should be seriously explored. The purpose of these arrangements is not to freeze the status quo but to make a highly dynamic situation more stable.

"Serious dilemmas" encompassed in five dimensions that interim arrangements might be expected to address are described in detail: mutual reassurances regarding issues of greatest concern, development of cross-strait dialogue, expansion of cross-strait economic and cultural ties, expansion of Taiwan's role in the international community, and military confidence-building measures.

Tao Wenzhao, while objective in perspective, is less clinical in his chapter. Tao's "U.S. Policy Ambiguities and Current Cross-Strait Dilemmas" reminds the reader, specialist or generalist, of the deep emotion mainland China and Taiwan policy analysts attach to cross-strait issues.

For many mainland China and Taiwan analysts, cross-strait issues are not necessarily amenable to simple rational-actor allocations of competing interests. These issues represent vigorous thrusts and parries regarding China's territorial integrity and sovereignty. Some of the thrusts and parries are personal. Tao considers Taiwan President Lee Teng-hui's July 9, 1999, statement regarding PRC and Taiwan relations as constituting "special state-to-state relations" a "formal and undisguised challenge to the one-China principle" in a way "unprecedented in the history of cross-strait relations."

The criticism of Tao and others does not stop with President Lee. It extends to the "dual character and ambiguity of U.S. policy toward Taiwan." Tao reflects mainstream PRC belief that "the purpose of U.S. Taiwan policy is to keep the status quo," since, regarding Taiwan, "neither reunification nor independence is in the U.S. interest." Here revealed, however politely expressed, is a contentious divergence of perception regarding the fundamental interest and purpose between the United States and the PRC regarding Taiwan.

Moving from frameworks and ambiguities, we address a second issue: "one China" and international space.

"One China" refers to the ongoing tug-of-war over who defines China, including its legal legitimacy, territorial integrity, and national sovereignty. "International space" refers to a fundamental dilemma: Taipei says that Beijing should allow Taiwan to play an international role commensurate with its objective international standing as a sign of cross-strait goodwill and common interest. Beijing says that increasing Taiwan's international status will only intensify Taipei's demands and international sympathy for Taiwan independence.

The four chapters in this section provide balanced if dramatically divergent perspectives on Taiwan's participation in international organizations and Taiwan's legal status.

Loh I-cheng's sophisticated analysis of current polling data and other indicators of the democratic preferences of Taiwan's citizens asks a crucial question: Will the PRC's to-date successful diplomatic isolation of Taipei "achieve exactly the opposite of the PRC's declared objective of eventual unification of the two Chinas"? Loh's hope is for both sides to "take a step backward and find the sky and sea so much wider" (*tui yi bu hai kuo tian kung*). In Loh's view, only this larger perspective may cut the Gordian knot "that inextricably ties cross-strait relations to public sentiment in Taiwan and save the Chinese nation from a prolonged period of forced separation."

While Loh calls for mutual cross-strait accommodation, Chu Shulong argues that it is Taipei, not Beijing, that keeps disrupting a workable and working "one-China" status quo. "What worries Beijing," Chu asserts, "is that Taiwan wants to go beyond its international boundary," a phenomenon particularly associated with the past 10 years and confirmed correct, in Chu's mind, by Lee's "two-state theory." Two solutions proposed by Chu are maintaining a "one-China" framework and the status quo while asking for three new no's: no new crises, no incautious responses, and no support or encouragement for those creating trouble across the strait.

Similarly, for his perspective, Zhao Gancheng argues why the reasons Taiwan generally gives for seeking more international space are understandable but erroneous. He tackles head-on Taipei's contention that two historically separate entities exist because the PRC never ruled Taiwan, that Taiwan have equal status with the mainland in talks on political affairs, and that international dignity and space require greater international involvement, even while avoiding armed conflict or regulating competition short of conflict.

In a statement challenging both sides of the Taiwan Strait, Zhao calls for "wisdom and common sense by leaders across the strait," since "public opinion can be misleading." He warns that "propaganda by the two sides can only worsen the situation," and that the "over use of public opinion may undermine stability and the ability to promote a peaceful solution to the issue." How to reconcile appeals to leaders with volatile if democratic public opinion is clearly a delicate cross-strait dilemma.

Creatively examining democratic sovereignty in international law, Philip Yang considers the meaning of "one China" and relations between the two political entities across the Taiwan Strait. As if to emphasize the different perspectives on Taiwan's status across the Taiwan Strait, Yang expounds an interlocking set of domestic and international legal reasons why, in his view, "though bilateral political and private law relations remain unique and special circumstances apply, China and Taiwan are, in political and legal reality, two separate states."

This argument explains, in a reasoned and rational way starting from a certain set of premises and logic, President Lee's claim that stating mainland China and Taiwan constitute "special state-to-state relations" is only to reiterate an existing status quo, not to declare Taiwan's independence either directly or incrementally.

The conventional wisdom that cross-strait economics bind whereas cross-strait politics separate is put into more complex context in the third section on economic dependencies and interdependencies.

Gary Jefferson draws on models of product cycles and quality that focus on interactions between innovative firms in the "north" and imitators in the "south" to argue that Taiwan's continuing prosperity will "require political accommodation with the mainland." "It is not possible," Jefferson concludes, "to sustain the current condition of economic integration and political disintegration."

Using Taiwan's personal computer industry as an example, Jefferson envisages two possibilities: Taiwan moves upstream by creating its own brands; alternatively, Taiwan integrates vertically with mainland suppliers, as U.S. and Japanese multinationals are attempting to do. Either or some combination of both strategies puts a premium on Taiwan's reducing its economic vulnerability to political instability "which provides the mainland with a strategic policy instrument."

Wang Jianmin focuses on trade and investment opportunities presented by the possible upcoming entry of both the PRC and Taiwan into the World Trade Organization (WTO). Wang's optimistic economic scenarios see cross-strait trade and investment burgeoning, as Taiwan seizes new openings to expand into the mainland's interior market in the telecommunications, tourism, foreign trade, wholesale, and retail sectors.

Wang also cites high-tech, securities, and insurance industries as possible new and leading areas of cross-strait economic cooperation, itself only part of a larger accelerating economic integration of the China region, including mainland China, Hong Kong, and Taiwan.

Similarly, but reflecting the perspective of a Taipei wary of Beijing's political stick rather than one enticed by Beijing's economic carrot, Lee-in Chen Chiu analyzes Taiwan's investment policies. She includes Taipei's division of labor across the Taiwan Strait during the 1978–1986 period of trade inception and the post-1987 period of investment inception.

She reviews the economic and political logic behind key Taiwan statutes and regulations legalizing economic interaction across the strait. She also presents detailed figures to show how Taiwan contributed to regional stability during the Asian financial crisis by maintaining foreign direct investment, including through Taipei's diverse industrial networks.

In the final section, contingencies and dilemmas are considered.

As 2000 begins, the conventional wisdom is that Taiwan remains perhaps intractably rooted in history. Yet past patterns and agreements, even dynamic status quos, seem increasingly challenged to maintain peace, prosperity, and stability in the Taiwan Strait in the future.

And globalization brings new challenges. Who would have imagined that Beijing, Moscow, and others would link modern conflict over ancient confrontation in Kosovo or Chechnya to Taiwan's international status, as reflected in President Jiang Zemin's declaration that "Taiwan is not Kosovo"? In this perspective, the complex circumstances at the time underscore why it is not in the interest of either the PRC or the United States for the May 7, 1999 (Belgrade time), bombing of the PRC embassy in Belgrade to become a modern example in China's litany of historic humiliations.

Chiou I-jen logically considers the sources of the stalemate in cross-strait relations as a "prisoner's dilemma." In game theory, he explains, a prisoner's dilemma arises when, although not in the best interest of either side, distrust and lack of mutual confidence lead to confrontation.

Chiou then analyzes the cross-strait military, diplomatic, and economic dilemmas. He underscores how the benefits of mutual cooperation "whether in the form of trade profits, military confidence building, or cost savings on the diplomatic battlefield" may, from the inside, still be insufficient to transcend "internal insecurities, suspicions, emotional contradictions necessary to reach the trust needed for mutual compromise."

So, even while recognizing the dilemma that both sides "will adamantly oppose a U.S.-brokered political agreement," Chiou still argues that only the United States can play a useful—and needed—outside "guarantor" role to facilitate, implement, and enforce cross-strait agreements. The underlying rationale for this conclusion parallels those in the opening chapter of this report.

Nancy Tucker considers how specific (and sometimes unpredictable) contingency developments may affect cross-strait dynamics. Military contingencies include possible PRC military action, theater missile defense issues, and dynamic military balances challenged by PRC military modernization.

In the economic area, one the one hand, Tucker can imagine the PRC's inability to cope with bankrupt, state-owned enterprises; insolvent banking systems; overbuilt property markets; unemployment; and regional economic disparities creating economic crisis. On the other hand, she can also imagine the entry of the PRC and Taiwan into the WTO "substantially changing cross-strait economic relations." The domestic politics of Taiwan, the United States, and the PRC also add uncertainties, as would regional disorder arising from destabilizing developments in Korea or Hong Kong.

All this brings us and this volume full circle. Our intellectual and policy journey has traversed four key issues. It has considered in turn frameworks and ambiguities, "one China" and international space, economic dependencies and interdependencies, and contingencies and dilemmas. These themes illustrate the panoply of Taiwan Strait issues through which Beijing, Taipei, and Washington must navigate in the new century.

From a Washington policy perspective, the U.S. government has enunciated a series of fundamental principles as issues in the Taiwan Strait have evolved. These U.S. policy principles include

- clear and consistent reaffirmation of the U.S. one-China policy as defined by the three communiqués;

- insistence that the Taiwan Strait issue be resolved peacefully;

- continued arms sales to Taiwan, pursuant to the Taiwan Relations Act, to ensure that the island's armed forces have sufficient self-defense capability;

- confidence that the two sides have the creativity to resolve issues on their own, without U.S. government mediation;

- refusal to pressure either side to accept any arrangements it does not believe are in its interests;

- understanding that any arrangements between Beijing and Taipei should be on a mutually acceptable basis, not imposed by one side on the other;

- understanding that because Taiwan is a democracy, any arrangement between the two sides ultimately has to be acceptable to the Taiwan public; and finally

- willingness to support any outcome voluntarily agreed to by both sides of the Taiwan Strait.[1]

As 2000 opens a new century, delicate policy balances remain in the face of continuing Taiwan Strait dilemmas. Thus the United States remains committed to policy principles that encourage direct dialogue (and discourage efforts to talk through Washington), thus focusing responsibility for mutual problem solving by the two sides of the Taiwan Strait themselves. At the same time, the United States seeks to retain policy principles sufficiently flexible to protect and advance U.S. interests in changing circumstances by forestalling, as necessary, possible cross-strait crises, while avoiding U.S. intervention or mediation.

Indeed, it is our intent and hope that this analytical presentation of Taiwan Strait dilemmas as they involve Beijing–Taipei–Washington policies in the new century will leave a clear sense that small steps are being taken, but much remains to be done.

Notes

1. Richard C. Bush, chairman and managing director, American Institute in Taiwan, "United States Policy Towards Taiwan," Joint Conference of the USA/ROC and ROC/USA Business Councils, San Antonio, Tex., November 19, 1999, p. 3.

ACKNOWLEDGMENTS

IT IS UNUSUAL to bring together leading experts—all with strongly held views—from the People's Republic of China, Taiwan, and the United States to discuss the real, thorny policy issues and conclude with a better understanding regarding themselves and those issues. Therefore, I first acknowledge and express appreciation for the professionalism displayed by each of the participants in this endeavor, including for making the effort to gather and produce something constructive. Richard Bush, chairman and managing director of the American Institute in Taiwan, spoke with the group at its 1999 meeting and kindly wrote the foreword to this, the resulting volume. David Robinson of the IMF and U.S. Representative Matt Salmon (R-Ariz.), although not represented in the volume, gave keynote presentations to the group, allowing it to examine relevant issues from multiple dimensions and perspectives. Former secretaries of defense Harold Brown and James Schlesinger, CSIS counselors, who always provide valuable policy perspective and insight, reviewed the volume in manuscript and provided comments for the book's back cover.

Nor do endeavors such as this evolve into publishable books without dedicated professional effort. In this regard, I thank James Dunton, Mary Marik, Pamela Mills, and others at The CSIS Press for working closely with me and the CSIS Asia Program to produce this volume in a timely way.

Throughout this effort, Philip Liu, research associate in the CSIS Asia Program, has worked with determination and skill to help shape the discussion agenda, to follow up with the substantive and administrative details, and generally to bring this project to fruition.

PART ONE

FRAMEWORKS AND AMBIGUITIES

CHAPTER ONE

AGAIN ON INTERIM ARRANGEMENTS IN THE TAIWAN STRAIT

Harry Harding

ONE OF THE MOST CONTROVERSIAL ASPECTS of the Taiwan issue in the past several months has been the concept of some kind of mutually acceptable framework for relations between Taiwan and the People's Republic of China (PRC), and for Taiwan's place in the international community, during the long interim before the ultimate status of Taiwan can be determined.

Proponents of this concept have used different terms at different times to refer to what they have in mind. Some have described them as interim agreements, others as a modus vivendi, still others as mechanisms for peace and stability. Perhaps the most generic term is the one I use here: interim arrangements. I use the word "arrangements" rather than "agreements" to suggest that they need not necessarily be formal written compacts but may be embodied in parallel statements, tacit understandings, or any other conceivable form.

The concept of interim arrangements is based on three key assumptions:

- The present situation in the Taiwan Strait is unstable, although it possesses many more elements of mutual interdependence than it did 15 years ago.

- A final resolution of the Taiwan question is inconceivable in the short to medium term, given the different levels of development of the two economies, the differences in their political systems, the low level of mutual trust, and the inability thus far to find a formula acceptable to both sides.

- Therefore, given the impossibility of a final resolution of the question anytime soon, and given the dangers of instability, some kind of interim arrangement should be seriously explored.

The purpose of these arrangements is not to freeze the status quo but to make a highly dynamic situation more stable.

CONCEPT OF INTERIM ARRANGEMENTS

The concept of interim arrangements is not new. A tacit and incomplete set of interim arrangements has been in place, and evolving, since the two sides began to expand their economic and social relations in the late 1980s and started their quasi-official dialogue in the early 1990s. The U.S. interest in promoting interim arrangements can be dated to the mid-1980s when Secretary of State George Shultz supported expanded cross-strait relations.

But the topic has become more salient and aroused greater controversy since the Taiwan Strait crisis of 1995–1996. At that time, Taiwan's president, Lee Teng-hui, obtained a visa to attend a meeting at his alma mater, Cornell University. The PRC saw this successful effort as a significant step toward Taiwanese independence and a sign of U.S. support for such a move. The results were the suspension of the quasi-official cross-strait dialogue and China's engaging in a series of military exercises, including missile firings off the coast of Taiwan, to display its displeasure. To show its own commitment to a peaceful future for Taiwan, the United States moved two aircraft carrier battle groups into the area in the spring of 1996.

During and after the crisis, several U.S. analysts, including some who were former government officials and one who subsequently joined government service, encouraged the resumption of dialogue across the Taiwan Strait and the construction of a more stable set of cross-strait relationships that could prevent such a crisis from recurring. Then, in April 1999, Assistant Secretary of State Stanley Roth, in a speech on the twentieth anniversary of the Taiwan Relations Act, endorsed what he called interim agreements between Taiwan and the PRC.

Such proposals attracted great attention, and harsh criticism, on Taiwan. Indeed, one reason that Lee Teng-hui introduced the so-called two-state theory (*liang guo lun*) in an interview with the German radio station Deutsche Welle in July 1999 was apparently to forestall further U.S. pressure for interim agreements.

The objections expressed on Taiwan did not reflect a rejection of the concept of interim arrangements per se. After all, President Lee himself proposed the creation of "mechanisms for cross-strait peace and stability," a form of interim arrangement. Instead, Taipei's concerns reflected deep suspicion of U.S. policy toward Taiwan. Specifically, they embodied the apprehension that interim arrangements designed in the United States would inevitably favor the interests of the PRC over those of Taiwan.

Taiwan's suspicions of the United States in turn were rooted in the following developments:

- After the tensions in the Taiwan Strait in 1995–1996, the U.S. government formulated the so-called three no's and articulated them increasingly publicly and increasingly authoritatively. The three no's were that the United States would not pursue a policy of "two Chinas" or "one China, one Taiwan," that it would not support Taiwan's independence, and that it would not support Taiwan's membership in international organizations that require statehood. None of these three no's represented a change in policy. But they were seen as a clear tilt toward Beijing. The third in particular was regarded in Taipei as a rejection of Taiwan's attempt to play a more active role in international affairs and as a violation of the provision of the Taiwan Relations Act saying that the United States would continue to support Taiwan's membership in international organizations.

- After the first public articulation of the three no's during Jiang Zemin's visit to the United States in 1997, Chinese analysts began to probe their U.S. counterparts to determine whether the PRC could obtain further "adjustments" in U.S. policy toward Taiwan. They suggested a moratorium on U.S. arms sales to Taiwan, assurances that the United States would not deploy theater missile defense systems to the island, exclusion of Taiwan from the scope of the U.S.-Japan Mutual Security Treaty, an explicit U.S. statement that it preferred the eventual unification of Taiwan and China, or even U.S. endorsement of the PRC's one-country, two-systems formula, in light of the successful return of Hong Kong to Chinese sovereignty. Officials and analysts on Taiwan worried that the interim arrangements proposed by the United States might be the mechanism by which those adjustments would be made.

■ These concerns were exacerbated by the one-sidedness of some of the specific proposals put forward by U.S. analysts. One in particular called both for a moratorium on discussions of unification and for a pledge that negotiations on unification would begin after the moratorium had expired. This was seen in Taiwan as reflecting a U.S. commitment to the eventual unification of Taiwan with China and as setting a deadline for negotiations similar to the deadline that the lease on the New Territories had set for negotiations on the future of Hong Kong.

Thus, in the spring of 1999, Taiwanese analysts and political leaders were sharply criticizing the concept of interim arrangements. They even charged that the U.S. suggestions in this regard violated some of the six reassurances that the United States had given Taiwan in August 1982 at the time of the arms sales communiqué between Washington and Beijing (e.g., that the United States would neither press for negotiations across the Taiwan Strait nor mediate between the two sides).

ASSESSING INTERIM ARRANGEMENTS

The first question in assessing the desirability of interim arrangements is whether they address a serious problem. I believe they do. Although, as noted above, cross-strait relations are far more extensive today than they were in the mid-1980s, they are not necessarily stable. I reach this judgment for the following reasons:

- The development of cross-strait commercial relations has stalled in part for economic reasons, the sluggish growth of the mainland economy in recent months. But it also reflects Taiwan's reluctance to reduce its restrictions on cross-strait transportation and economic ties.

- The two sides have each placed conditions on the resumption of political dialogue that are unacceptable to the other. Beijing insists that Taiwan accept the so-called one-China formula: There is one China, the PRC is the sole legitimate government of China, and Taiwan is part of China. Taiwan has now countered with the two-state theory: There may be one China again some day, but in the meantime the two sides should deal with each other as separate and equal states. In other words, Taiwan is insisting on an equal legal status with the PRC, which Beijing is reluctant to acknowledge.

- Both sides are growing impatient with the status quo. With the return of Macao to Chinese sovereignty in December 1999, the PRC may assign even higher priority to resolving the Taiwan question. At the same time, as the assertion of a distinct Taiwanese identity grows, many on Taiwan are dissatisfied with the restricted role that the island plays in the international community.

- Relatedly, both sides may be more worried that time is running out—or at least that it is not on their side. Analysts in Beijing must be concerned about a steady shift of identity on Taiwan, away from a sense of being Chinese toward a self-image as Taiwanese, and the related decline in support in public opinion polls for unification with the mainland. Conversely, analysts in Taipei are apprehensive about the eventual rise of Chinese power. Not only will this allow Beijing to exert various forms of coercion against Taiwan, but it may make the United States less willing to support Taiwan's initiatives or to defend it against the mainland.

- Finally, an arms race in the Taiwan Strait is possible. The PRC is developing the capability to put military pressure on Taiwan, not only through deployment of ballistic missiles but also through development of conventional air, naval, and amphibious forces. It also seeks the capability to deter the United States from intervening in a crisis on Taiwan's behalf. For its part, the United States is considering deployment of theater missile defense systems to Taiwan to counter the PRC's missile deployments. And some in Taiwan talk about the need for developing counteroffensive capabilities if the island is to deter or defend against an attack by the mainland.

Two crises over cross-strait relations since 1995—the controversy over Lee Teng-hui's visit to the United States in 1995 and the recent dispute over his two-states theory—are ample evidence of the possibility of instability in the Taiwan Strait. That the first crisis gave rise to military exercises and deployments by China and the United States and that some Chinese still talk of using force to deal with the second crisis indicate that the consequences of this instability could be profound. Thus a set of interim arrangements that reduce this instability benefits all parties.

DESIGNING INTERIM ARRANGEMENTS

But what would such interim arrangements look like? Can they be designed in ways acceptable to both sides? Five elements might be part of a comprehensive set of interim arrangements. These elements were originally contained in a paper I presented in Taipei earlier this year,[1] but the objective now is less to advocate these five ideas than to use them to analyze the feasibility and desirability of interim arrangements. Those who wish to design interim arrangements must address some serious dilemmas on each of these dimensions.

Set of Mutual Reassurances on the Basic Issues

A first assumption is that, to be effective, a set of interim arrangements must address in mutually acceptable fashion the issues of greatest concern on both sides. The mainland is concerned that Taiwan will declare independence from China. Taiwan is apprehensive that the mainland will use military force, or other forms of coercion, to compel it to accept unification on Beijing's terms. A set of interim arrangements that deal only with secondary issues, without touching on these more fundamental problems, will not be complete.

One possibility—indeed one suggested in my earlier paper and frequently mentioned by others—is that there could be a set of mutual, conditional reassurances on these two points. That is, the mainland would commit itself not to use force against Taiwan as long as Taiwan did not declare independence, and Taiwan would foreswear a unilateral declaration of independence as long as the mainland did not employ coercion to impose unification. The advantages of such an approach are clear:

- It addresses the issues of fundamental concern to each side.

- It does so in a balanced manner: An assurance by Taiwan is linked to a parallel assurance by the mainland.

- It also does so in a conditional way: The PRC would not renounce the use of force unconditionally, but only if Taiwan does not provoke that use of force by a declaration of independence. Similarly, Taiwan does not renounce a unilateral declaration of independence unconditionally, but does so only if the mainland continues to pursue unification by peaceful means.

- Finally, this approach is relatively feasible because it builds on existing trends. The PRC, although refusing to renounce the right to use force, has been increasingly willing to specify a narrow range of circumstances in which it would do so, the most important of which is precisely a unilateral declaration of independence by Taiwan. Indeed, Beijing has said it would agree to a cessation of hostilities if Taiwan accepted the one-China principle. Conversely, Taiwanese political leaders have increasingly acknowledged that a unilateral declaration of independence would be unnecessary and counterproductive, given the island's current autonomy from mainland rule and the likelihood that it would trigger the use of force by the mainland.

But there is a dilemma. Some Taiwanese leaders, renouncing the idea of a unilateral declaration, add that they can do so because Taiwan is already independent and no formal declaration is necessary. At the same time, public opinion polls on Taiwan reveal that support for unification, and the public's degree of self-identification as Chinese, is at an all-time low. This suggests that the threat to stability is not so much that Taiwan will unilaterally try to change the status quo but that it will unilaterally try to freeze it.

This in turn focuses attention on another situation Beijing has occasionally mentioned as a possible trigger for its use of force: a "protracted refusal to negotiate" on the part of Taiwan. It is increasingly this scenario, rather than a unilateral declaration of independence by Taipei, that an interim arrangement in the Taiwan Strait must successfully address.

One obvious way of approaching this issue is a moratorium on negotiation for a long period of time, followed by an agreement to negotiate the terms of unification at some future point, but it seems unrealistic. Beijing will not want a long moratorium on the issue; Taiwan will want neither a deadline for negotiations nor an agreement in advance on the ultimate outcome of those negotiations.

Rather, a different framework for dealing with this issue might include the following:

- Taiwan would continue to keep unification on the table—as a possible, even preferred, outcome—even while justifiably insisting that certain preconditions will have to be met if unification is to be achieved. For all the controversy surrounding it, Lee Teng-hui's interview with Deutsche Welle did precisely this.

- The PRC would acknowledge that preconditions for unification have not been met and that serious negotiations on this issue are infeasible in the foreseeable future. It would also have to acknowledge, at least tacitly, that the main challenge will be to persuade Taiwan of the desirability of unification, not merely to devise acceptable formulas by which unification might be achieved.

Development of Cross-Strait Dialogue

The second element in a comprehensive set of interim arrangements would be the expansion of cross-strait dialogue on political as well as technical issues. In my earlier paper, I suggested that the nature of this dialogue could be expected to evolve over time. At first, its principal purpose would be simply to enhance mutual understanding: to help people on the mainland understand the rising sense of local identity on Taiwan and to help people on Taiwan understand the importance the mainland attaches to unification. Over time, the dialogue might evolve to exploring the feasibility of unification, including preconditions, and the various formulas that might ultimately prove acceptable to the two sides. The dialogue might eventually become a formal negotiation on these issues.

This dialogue should involve not just the current discussions between representatives of the Straits Exchange Foundation (SEF) and the Association for Relations Across the Taiwan Strait (ARATS). It should also involve Track Two channels for discussion that could involve broader participation by influential people on both sides, especially the various political parties on Taiwan. This reflects the fact that, in Asia, Track Two dialogue is a well-established way of dealing with sensitive issues in a responsible but informal manner, and that broader participation would help build the political base on Taiwan for a redefined relationship with the mainland, whether an interim or a final arrangement.

This second element in an interim arrangement is in many ways increasingly feasible. The ARATS–SEF channel is already a form of Track Two dialogue, although (as just noted) it needs to be expanded. There are now many forums for dialogue between policy analysts from the mainland and Taiwan. The Taiwanese government's position has steadily evolved from the "no-contact" policy of the 1980s, to an insistence on discussing only "technical" issues, to a conditional willingness to engage in political dialogue.

There are also several dilemmas here that need to be openly acknowledged and seriously addressed. For example, we should not be naive about the results of dialogue. Dialogue can build mutual understanding, identify common interests, and produce innovative ideas for solving problems. But dialogue can also reveal the depth of mistrust, the differences in interest, and the gaps between the policy preferences of the participants. It is always possible therefore that dialogue can make a situation worse rather than better. Moreover, although governments increasingly give lip service to Track Two dialogue, they remain highly suspicious of high-level exchanges they cannot control.

An even bigger obstacle to cross-strait dialogue exists not at the Track Two level but at the Track One, or official, level. The principal message contained in Lee Teng-hui's interview with Deutsche Welle was that, in any official dialogue, Taiwan would insist on being treated as the mainland's equal. In Lee's words, it would reject being categorized as a "province" (or other local government), let alone a "renegade province."

In fact, the mainland has already promised to deal with Taiwan on the basis of "equality," so one could argue that the two sides have already agreed in principle on this question. But finding an operational definition of an equal, official relationship will not be easy. The PRC has offered to deal with the president of Taiwan as the leader of the ruling party (the Kuomintang) on a par with the leader of the mainland's ruling party (the CCP [Chinese Communist Party]). Indeed, it was in the capacity of general secretary of the CCP that Jiang Zemin met with Koo Chen-fu during the latter's visit to Beijing in 1998. But it is very difficult for a multiparty system such as Taiwan's to engage in official discussions on a party-to-party basis. And it begs the question as to the nature of the government on Taiwan, which presumably would have to convert formal agreements between the two sides into legal form.

Lee Teng-hui's solution was that the two sides regard the situation as a "special form of state-to-state relations." Whatever the ambiguities of the English version of his remarks, the phrase used in Chinese, *guo yu guo guanxi*, implies country-to-country relations. And the notion that cross-strait relations are international, rather than intranational, in character is completely unacceptable to the mainland.

From an outside perspective, the obvious solution is to define the relationship between the two sides as a government-to-government relationship within a nation divided by an inconclusive civil war. That, before announcement of the *liang guo lun*, was the essence of Taiwan's position. But that formula has at least three implications that so far Beijing has refused to accept: There is a legitimate government on Taiwan (Beijing refers only to the Taiwan "authorities"), that government is sovereign over the territory it controls (Beijing refers only to "jurisdiction"), and that government is headed by a president (Beijing refers only to a "leader"). It will not be easy to bridge these remaining gaps, which are key to creating an official cross-strait dialogue on equal terms or even to permitting meetings between Lee Teng-hui or his successor and mainland representatives such as Wang Daohan.

Expansion of Cross-Strait Economic and Cultural Ties

A third element in any comprehensive set of interim arrangements would be the further expansion of cross-strait economic and cultural ties, including establishment of more direct transportation and communications links (the so-called *santong*) and the relaxation of remaining barriers to trade and investment. Such a development would be in the economic interests of both parties. From a political perspective, it would meet the demands of business communities on both sides of the Taiwan Strait. Moreover, in the longer run, these enhanced links between the two societies help enhance mutual understanding, build interdependence that can prevent conflict, and promote economic development of the mainland, which is one (although not the only) precondition for unification.

What then is the dilemma? The most obvious problem is that Taiwan has used the expansion of cross-strait economic links, especially the *santong*, as a bargaining chip in its tacit negotiations with Beijing. Specifically, Taipei has sought a renunciation of force, or a cessation of hostilities, as the precondition for the inauguration of the *santong*. This problem can best be resolved by seeing the expansion of cross-strait ties as part of a comprehensive package of interim arrangements, including the mutual reassurances discussed above.

But there is also a deeper problem: Taipei's fear that growing economic links will create an asymmetrical form of interdependence that makes Taiwan more vulnerable to the mainland than the mainland is to Taiwan. It is clear that the issue is not the type or direction of the economic relationship. Taiwanese leaders and analysts seem to worry not only that their investments on the mainland are making them vulnerable to pressure from Beijing but also that mainland investment on Taiwan would do the same. (Logically these two types of investment should have parallel and reciprocal consequences.) Rather, the issue seems to be Taiwan's concern that the authoritarian nature of politics on the mainland makes economic sanctions (or economic pressure more generally) a tool that is easier for Beijing to use than for Taipei to use.

The challenge then is to find ways to reassure Taiwan that growing economic interdependence does not produce asymmetrical vulnerabilities. One approach might be for the two sides to agree to apply the rules of the World Trade Organization (WTO) to each other, once they are both members. That would reduce the ability of both sides to exercise economic pressure against the other and make many attempts to do so a violation of a multilateral international obligation.

Expansion of Taiwan's Role in the International Community

One of Taiwan's principal objectives in recent years has been to expand the range and formality of its international relationships. Taipei argues correctly that it has much to offer the international community, from financial capital to technical advice. But the main reason for this strand in Taiwanese policy is to enable the people of Taiwan to have a sense of international identity they now lack.

Thus far, this issue has been a serious sticking point in cross-strait relations and an arena for sharp competition between the two sides in the international community. Beijing has stymied Taiwan's attempts to join various intergovernmental organizations including the World Health Organization and the United Nations. The PRC has successfully kept Taiwan from securing dual recognition from other nations (most notably from South Korea and South Africa). Taiwan and the mainland engage in an ongoing (and costly) competition to secure diplomatic recognition from smaller states (such as Papua New Guinea, Macedonia, and Panama). From an international perspective, Lee Teng-hui's *liang guo lun* is a plea both for dual recognition by the international community and for dual representation in intergovernmental organizations, as well as for equal and official relations across the Taiwan Strait. But that aspect of the *liang guo lun* has also been rejected by Beijing.

The situation, although difficult, is not without hope.

First, there is now ample precedent for Taiwan's membership in international organizations in which membership is not restricted to sovereign states. Taiwan has been able to join first the Asian Development ment Bank, then APEC (Asia-Pacific Economic Cooperation), and now the WTO, although the name by which it has done so has not always been agreeable.

Second, Beijing has said that, if Taiwan would only accept the one-China principle, a further expansion of its international activities would be "negotiable." This begs two obvious questions:

- What would constitute acceptance of the one-China principle? Would the kinds of mutual reassurances outlined above—in which Taiwan would agree to keep the possibility of unification on the table—be satisfactory?

- What kind of expansion of Taiwan's activities could Beijing accept? Could there ever be agreement on Taiwan's membership in intergovernmental organizations alongside the PRC, as the two Germanys and the two Koreas were able to do? Could there ever be agreement on dual recognition, again using the precedent (which Beijing itself adopted) of diplomatic relations with both Bonn and East Berlin, both Pyongyang and Seoul?

A step short of dual representation would be for Taiwan to participate in international organizations in some capacity other than that as a nation-state. Given the greater range of actors acknowledged to be key players in international affairs—from Hong Kong to the Palestinian Liberation Organization to multinational corporations to nongovernment organizations—there will over time be growing precedents for creative minds to consider in defining Taiwan's involvement in the international community. Indeed there is an intriguing paradox: Taiwan is insisting on sovereign status at a time when sovereignty in international affairs is becoming increasingly blurred.

Military Confidence-Building Measures

Finally, a comprehensive set of interim arrangements would also include various confidence-building measures between the military establishments of the two sides. These might include the following:

- Communication and other channels of coordination between the two sides that can allow peaceful interaction and deal with military incidents. For example, opening direct air and shipping links between the two sides will also require some mechanism for coordinated monitoring of civilian traffic in and above the Taiwan Strait. Hot lines—coupled with direct military-to-military dialogue—will make it possible to deal constructively with any incident.

- Restrictions on maneuvers and exercises that could lead to war by accident. The provocative aerial exercises over the Taiwan Strait in recent months show the importance of this aspect of military confidence building.

- Above all, restrictions on competitive military deployments that could produce a costly and dangerous arms race in the Taiwan Strait. In particular, there is an obvious potential trade-off between the PRC's deployment of ballistic missiles opposite Taiwan and the deployment of theater missile defense systems by either Taiwan or the United States.

- Because the level of U.S. arms sales to Taiwan is linked to the military balance in the Taiwan Strait, restrictions on the PRC's military deployments could lead to comparable limits on U.S. arms sales to Taiwan.

The mutual reassurances that lie at the heart of any interim arrangements will lay the groundwork for these kinds of continental ballistic missiles. But they will not make them easy. They will be complicated by three facts: that the PRC will not issue an unconditional use of force, that neither side will completely forgo military preparations, and that the United States will continue arms sales to Taiwan. It will be impossible to envisage a secure community in the Taiwan Strait where the use of force is inconceivable and preparations for war are unnecessary. It may be possible for the various parties to exercise greater restraint in acquiring and deploying arms and in the size and character of their military exercises.

ROLE OF THE UNITED STATES

What would be the U.S. role in any set of interim arrangements in the Taiwan Strait? Analysts in Taiwan sometimes make two arguments on this subject that may at first blush appear contradictory: They regard direct U.S. involvement in any negotiation as illegitimate, but they want the United States to guarantee any interim arrangements that may be devised.

Taiwan's objection to U.S. involvement reflects in part the concerns outlined above: the fear that U.S. involvement will inevitably be biased in favor of the PRC's interests at the expense of Taiwan's, whether because of China's greater power or because of U.S. alleged romanticism about Beijing. Taiwanese analysts also point out that any U.S. attempt to mediate the Taiwan Strait dispute would violate assurances that Washington gave Taipei in 1982, that the United States would not engage in mediation between the two sides.

As the late Gerald Segal of the International Institute for Strategic Studies once pointed out, the dispute in the Taiwan Strait appears to be the only foreign conflict that the United States has said, as a matter of principle, it will never mediate. But, however unique, that is indeed U.S. policy. The current U.S. promotion of interim arrangements is not a form of mediation aimed at producing a substantive solution to the Taiwan Strait issue. Rather it is a way to encourage greater stability in the Taiwan Strait during the long interim before such a solution can conceivably be reached.

But what about a U.S. guarantee of interim arrangements? Some Taiwanese analysts have drawn a parallel with the U.S. guarantee of the Camp David agreements of 1979 and asked whether the United States would issue a similar guarantee for the Taiwan Strait.

There are two important points about the U.S. guarantee in the Middle East.[2] The United States had just mediated the Camp David accords, a much more intensive role than anyone expects the United

States to play in creating interim agreements in the Taiwan Strait. And the guarantee was quite vague. It promised to provide aerial monitoring of the situation on the ground and to promote the creation of some kind of multilateral peacekeeping force. In the event of an actual or threatened violation of the peace treaty, the United States promised only to "consult with the Parties . . . and take such other actions as it may deem appropriate and helpful."

One could argue that the existing U.S. policy toward the Taiwan Strait provides a tacit guarantee for any set of interim arrangements the two sides might reach. In particular, the Taiwan Relations Act would imply that any attempt by the PRC to use coercion in violation of the terms of such arrangements would be of grave concern to the United States. And certainly the United States would also expect Taiwan to fulfill obligations under any interim arrangements with the mainland.

Ultimately, one objective of interim arrangements should be to reduce the degree of U.S. involvement in the Taiwan issue. Each side is now negotiating with the other through Washington, trying to mobilize support for its own policy positions while portraying the other as a troublemaker. Under pressure from both sides, the United States often seems to vacillate, tilting first in one direction (granting a visa to Lee Teng-hui to visit Cornell University) and then in the other (issuing the three no's). This simply encourages the two sides to appeal to the United States for support rather than deal with each other more directly.

Although the main purpose of interim arrangements is to produce stability, increase mutual understanding, and enhance interdependence across the Taiwan Strait, another is to end this dynamic. The two sides should be dealing—hopefully more constructively and cooperatively—with each other, rather than through the United States. If so, although the United States will still play a stabilizing role in the Taiwan Strait, in other respects its role in cross-strait relations can become far more secondary than has been true thus far.

Notes

1. Harry Harding, "Toward a Modus Vivendi in the Taiwan Strait," paper prepared for the Conference on U.S.-Taiwan Relations: Twenty Years After the Taiwan Relations Act, sponsored by the Institute of European and American Studies, Academia Sinica, Taipei, April 9–10, 1999.

2. The text of the guarantee, conveyed in identical letters sent by President Carter to President Sadat and Prime Minister Begin, is in William B. Quandt, *Camp David: Peacemaking and Politics* (Washington: Brookings, 1986), 406.

CHAPTER TWO

U.S. POLICY AMBIGUITIES AND CURRENT CROSS-STRAIT DILEMMAS

Tao Wenzhao

THE SUCCESSFUL VISIT TO THE MAINLAND OF KOO CHEN-FU, chairman of the Straits Exchange Foundation (SEF), in October 1998, sparked some hope for the future of cross-strait relations. Consensus between him and Wang Daohan, head of the Association for Relations Across the Taiwan Strait (ARATS), was reached in four areas: (1) a return visit to Taiwan by Wang Daohan, originally scheduled for the autumn of 1999; (2) further dialogue on political, economic, and other issues; (3) more exchanges between SEF and ARATS; and (4) greater assistance for those visiting the mainland, and those visiting Taiwan.

Then suddenly, without warning, Lee Teng-hui made his well-known statement on state-to-state relations to a German journalist on July 9, 1999. Consequently, the atmosphere for cross-strait relations deteriorated severely. Now concerned individuals from the mainland, Taiwan, and the United States are focusing on how to escape the dilemmas in the Taiwan issue.

LEE TENG-HUI, A TROUBLEMAKER

Since Lee Teng-hui became Taiwan's "president," the political situation on the island has undergone profound changes. Cross-strait relations have evolved from the original legal dispute as to "who represents 'one China'" to disputes over legal issues as they relate to "two Chinas" or "one China, one Taiwan."

There have been three serious cross-strait disputes in the past five years.

The first was triggered by Lee Teng-hui's conversation with Japanese right-wing author Ryotaro Shiba in March 1994. While discussing "the sorrow of the Taiwan people," Lee ascribed the source of sorrow to the mainland and challenged the concept of "China," alleging that reunification was only "strange sleep-talking." Throughout the conversation Lee compared himself with Moses of the Old Testament who led the Israelites across the Red Sea and back to their homeland. He even made clear his desire to see Taiwan established as a country. Quite naturally, his splittist statements provoked vigorous criticism from Taiwan, the mainland, Hong Kong, Macao, and overseas Chinese communities.

Lee's visit to the United States in June 1995 and his speech at Cornell University set off a second round of disputes in cross-strait relations.

Since July 1999, Lee Teng-hui has espoused the so-called seven-lump theory, which divides China into seven regions, and the two-state theory, setting off a third round of disputes in cross-strait relations. "Since we launched constitution reforms in 1991, we have defined cross-strait relations as state-to-state, or at least special state-to-state," said Lee. Such a formal and undisguised challenge to the one-China principle is unprecedented in the history of cross-strait relations.

The explanation of Koo Chen-fu and the statement issued by Taiwan's Mainland Affairs Council did not retract the two-state theory but defended Lee. Thus Lee Teng-hui caused the dilemmas in cross-strait relations.

TIMING OF LEE'S STATEMENT

The timing of Lee's announcement of his two-state theory was not accidental but based on the following factors.

- With Taiwan's "presidential elections" coming up in March 2000, Lee believes his time in office is limited. He wants to leave a political legacy. He is therefore counting on his two-state theory to set the tone for his successors and to maintain a Taiwanese administration sympathetic to his own ideals after his term is over.

- Lee intends to maneuver political developments in Taiwan before the spring 2000 election to gain advantage for the KMT (Kuomintang) candidate. He is not sure that Lien Chan will win the election. By advocating the two-state theory, Lee intends to influence the trend of political thought in Taiwan further in the direction of "independence" and, on the one hand, marginalize James Soong and, on the other hand, extend the Democratic Progressive Party's (DPP's) political space. By so doing he may win some ballots that would otherwise belong to James Soong or to Chen Shui-bian.

- With the improved atmosphere in cross-strait relations after Koo's visit to the mainland in October 1998, it seemed likely that cross-strait dialogue, especially dialogue on political matters, could begin. Lee did not want this development. He was afraid of the repercussions of Wang Daohan's visit. By making his state-to-state relationship announcement, Lee deliberately damaged the process of cross-strait dialogue and poisoned the environment of cross-strait talks, making Wang Daohan's visit to Taiwan impossible.

- With Sino-U.S. relations at their lowest point as a result of NATO's U.S.-led bombing of the Chinese embassy in Yugoslavia, Lee found a good opportunity to make trouble with his two-state theory.

After all, he deeply resents the one-China policy of the United States and especially the three no's made public by President Clinton during his China visit in the summer of 1998. He laid a trap for Sino-U.S. relations. He knew that the mainland could only respond strongly to his theory. But if the PRC response seemed too strong to the United States, Congress would probably pass the Taiwan Security Enhancement Act. Then Sino-U.S. relations would deteriorate further. Obviously, sabotaging Sino-U.S. relations is one of Lee's intentions. The situation is, as some U.S. scholars put it, one where "one tail wags two dogs."

CAUSING TROUBLE FOR THE UNITED STATES

When President Clinton met with President Jiang Zemin in Auckland on September 11, 1999, Clinton said the two-state remarks of Lee Teng-hui "had brought about a lot of troubles" for both China and the United States. The Clinton administration certainly does not like Lee Teng-hui's two-state theory. And differences in attitude toward Lee's statement exist between the administration and Congress, among congressional members, and in public opinion.

The Clinton administration's response to Lee's statement is different from its attitude toward Lee's 1995 U.S. visit. The administration responded quickly after the statement. President Clinton telephoned President Jiang to express the strong commitment of the United States to a one-China policy. U.S. officials, including Secretary of State Madeleine Albright and National Security Adviser Sandy Berger, reiterated that position on different occasions. Richard Bush, chairman of the American Institute in Taiwan, visited Taiwan where he asked Lee to explain what he meant. At the same time Stanley Roth, the assistant secretary of state, and Kenneth Lieberthal, the National Security Council's senior director for Asia, visited Beijing to reassure the Chinese government that U.S. policy had not changed. The most complete statement is Roth's National Press Club address in Australia. He expounded on the three pillars of U.S. policy:

First, the United States has made very clear its continued strong support for a one-China policy. There has been absolutely no change in U.S. policy. Second, the United States continues to emphasize the importance of direct negotiations between the parties. It is not up to the United States to be an intermediary or a mediator. The third, crucial pillar is the abiding interest that the United States has in a peaceful resolution of this issue and making sure that force is not used. At the summit in Oakland, President Clinton reiterated the one-China policy. Partly because of U.S. pressure Lee Teng-hui was compelled to announce that the state-to-state theory is "only [an] oral statement" and that he would not revise the "constitution" or related laws. Some members of Congress hold different views. Benjamin Gilman, chairman of the House International Relations Committee, visited Taiwan to express his support to Lee Teng-hui. In his announcement before leaving Taiwan, he praised Lee for speaking out on Taiwan's view of cross-strait relations and asserted that cross-strait dialogue should wait until China becomes a democracy.

Congress has always had divergent opinions, including those over China. Some members such as Jesse Helms and Ben Gilman support Lee's statement. But others criticize Lee's risky statement. Even Democratic Senator Robert Torricelli, who cosponsored the Taiwan Security Enhancement Act with Jesse Helms, criticized Lee for risking isolating Taiwan and triggering a confrontation with the mainland at the wrong time on the wrong basis.

Public opinion is also split over Lee's statement. It has been widely criticized by many China experts and former U.S. officials including Henry Kissinger, Zbigniew Brzezinski, Joseph Nye, and Brent Scowcroft. Michel Oksenberg called it a time bomb that could explode later. In contrast, some conservatives with the Heritage Foundation asked the United States to "defend Taiwan."

DUAL CHARACTER AND AMBIGUITY IN U.S. POLICY

The current trouble over Taiwan has been caused not only by Lee's state-to-state theory but also by the duality and ambiguity of U.S. policy toward Taiwan.

U.S. policy toward Taiwan has had a dual character since 1978 when the United States and China normalized relations. The policy is aimed at keeping a balance between the mainland and Taiwan, maintaining the current status of separation rather than reunification that the mainland strives for or independence that Lee Teng-hui and the DPP really intend to achieve. The Taiwan Relations Act (TRA) provides a new basis and legal framework for U.S.-Taiwan relations, allowing the United States to have a substantial relationship with Taiwan without official relations. When the United States and the PRC agreed in 1982 on the third communiqué on arms sales to Taiwan, the U.S. government made six assurances to Taiwan. It promised that the United States would not set a date for termination of arms sales to Taiwan, would not agree to hold prior consultation with the Chinese government on arms sales to Taiwan, would not alter the terms of the TRA, would not mediate between Taiwan and the mainland, would not alter its position on the sovereignty of Taiwan, and would not pressure Taiwan to negotiate with the mainland. Soon after President Clinton made public the three no's in the summer of 1998, the United States decided to sell more advanced weapons to Taiwan, including advanced frigates, antisubmarine S-2T aircraft, anti-air missiles, and E-2T early-warning aircraft.

Earlier in 1999, the United States hailed the twentieth anniversary of the TRA as a victory. On August 4, 1999, before the Senate Foreign Relations Committee, Kurt Campbell, deputy assistant secretary of defense, called the TRA "the most successful piece of legislative leadership in foreign policy in recent history."

On March 24, 1999, Stanley Roth noted that in the past 20 years "the TRA has not only helped to preserve the substance of our relationship with Taiwan, it has contributed to the conditions which have enabled the United States, the PRC, and Taiwan to achieve a great deal more." It is true that the TRA was carefully written, but the inherent ambiguity in the TRA is now a source of trouble for the United States. It is said that the U.S. decision to establish diplomatic relations with the PRC rests on the expectation that the future of Taiwan will be determined by peaceful means; indeed, in the TRA's words, the United States would "consider any effort to determine the future of Taiwan by other than peaceful means, including by boycotts or embargoes, a threat to the peace and security of the Western Pacific area and of grave concern to the United States."

Not said is what the United States would do if the situation described here happens. A great defect of the TRA is that it makes no distinction in situations not directly involving military force. And it does not ask whether all nonmilitary outcomes are themselves justified in determining the future of Taiwan. In this case the TRA simply provides Lee Teng-hui and those like him with an umbrella under which to go step by step toward the independence of Taiwan.

PURPOSE OF U.S. POLICY

One may ask the purpose of U.S. policy toward Taiwan. The TRA carefully avoided this question as if peace and stability in the western Pacific were the only concerns of the United States. Actually, U.S. policy is aimed at maintaining the status quo. Neither reunification nor independence is in the interest of the United States. The United States knows clearly that the mainland would not let Taiwan become independent. Taiwan's independence risks involving the United States militarily. The United States does not favor reunification for several reasons.

First, whether or not the United States has strategic interests in Taiwan (the United States often denies any strategic interest), Taiwan is now a good card for the United States to hold in dealing with both the mainland and Taiwan. Washington can conveniently play this card to pressure both Taiwan and the mainland. Second, some in the United States talk about the so-called China threat. When unification is realized, the comprehensive national strength of a greater China, including the mainland, Taiwan, Hong Kong, and Macao, will be far greater than that of China currently. In this event, China would be in a much stronger position to challenge the United States economically and militarily, or even to threaten its interests. To avoid this possibility, the United States hopes reunification will not occur.

On the one hand, there is some common ground between the policy of the United States and that of the PRC—neither supports independence. On the other hand, there is some divergence between them—one does not support reunification, whereas the other strives for it. Similarly, there is some common ground between the policy of the United States and that of Lee Teng-hui—neither supports reunification. There is again some divergence between them—one does not support independence, whereas the other strives for it. So U.S. policy does not completely satisfy either the mainland or Taiwan. In other words, the United States is caught between the mainland and Taiwan. That is the fundamental U.S. dilemma regarding Taiwan.

After Lee made his remarks, some members of Congress asked the administration to clarify the ambiguity and promise to protect Taiwan if the mainland were to use force to solve the Taiwan issue. Some advocated the Taiwan Security Enhancement Act. All this put the administration in a difficult position.

RESOLVING THE DILEMMAS

What can those on both sides of the strait and from the United States do to resolve the dilemmas?

1. Cross-strait relations need a new start. Lee is a troublemaker, a crisis maker, the greatest hindrance to cross-strait relations. The Chinese government has asked him to retract his two-state theory. Scholars understand that this would be difficult. So the two-state theory may be there as long as Lee is in power. The current dilemmas in cross-strait relations are likely to continue for a few months. The March 2000 general election in Taiwan gives some hope for the future. The new leader in Taiwan will not blindly follow his suit. Then Lee's statement will become irrelevant, providing a new start in cross-strait relations.

2. The mainland should remain calm and restrained. Naturally, those on the mainland are extremely dissatisfied with Lee's statement and have expressed their indignation. Some political and military pressure on Lee is also necessary to express the Chinese people's determination to protect their territorial integrity. Many are urging the government to respond strongly. But calm and restraint are needed for two reasons. First, although Lee's statement is a serious step toward independence, Taiwan is not yet independent. Although independence was written into the KMT's document, the constitution and relevant laws remain unchanged. Today it can be written into a document, tomorrow it can be deleted from the document. Second, as Taiwan's general election draws near, it is wise to watch carefully while refraining from exerting too much outside influence. We

should trust the Taiwanese and be confident that they will make a wise decision. Otherwise the result may be counterproductive.

3. The mainland should remain patient. There are two issues in cross-strait relations: reunification and opposition to Taiwan's independence. These two issues are connected. If Taiwan declares its independence, any talk about reunification will be meaningless. Nevertheless they remain distinct issues. Reunification will be a long process. Although China has general principles about reunification, it cannot be achieved in a short time. China needs to have more patience, even while opposing independence with urgency and determination. To do that China must show determination and will. Even then reunification will not be easy.

4. Cross-strait economic ties should be developed further. With Taiwanese commercial interests properly protected, cross-strait political talks should be started as soon as possible. South Korea two years ago expressed great envy as it watched the development of cross-strait economic relations. It is true that the two sides of the strait have achieved a great deal. Without cross-strait economic ties the general atmosphere in cross-strait relations would be much worse. Encouraging and strengthening cross-strait economic exchanges make Taiwan independence more difficult. Nevertheless it is wrong to think that economic relations naturally lead to political closeness, as past experience proves. Without improved cross-strait political relations, cross-strait economic ties remain limited and unsafe. Thus talks on political matters should start as soon as possible. Without such a start progress is impossible.

5. The United States should openly criticize Lee's two-state statement. Although U.S. officials, including President Clinton, repeat the U.S. commitment to a one-China policy, they refrain from saying they do not support Lee's statement. Thus pressure on Lee from the United States seems mild indeed.

6. The United States might impose some sanctions on Taiwan. Imposing sanctions is a common U.S. foreign policy practice and sometimes it makes sense. For example, the United States might postpone delivery of some weapons to Taiwan or suspend official visits at a certain level.

7. The United States should reconsider its arms sales to Taiwan from a long-term perspective. In spite of the third Sino-U.S. communiqué on August 17, 1982, the U.S. government continues to sell advanced weapons to Taiwan. During the past three years, U.S. arms sales to Taiwan have continued to increase in quantity and in quality. Such sales amounted to U.S.$1.163 billion in 1996, U.S.$1.172 billion in 1997, and U.S.$1.496 billion in 1998. Advanced weapons sold include the Patriot II missile, E-2 early-warning aircraft, and early-warning radar. Even after Lee's statement, the United States concluded a new deal with Taiwan on July 30, 1999, for a sum of U.S.$550 million. Past experience shows that the more advanced weapons the United States sells to Taiwan, the more reckless Lee Teng-hui becomes in planning and moving toward Taiwan independence. So arms sales to Taiwan become increasingly dangerous to cross-strait relations and to U.S. interests in the region. It is important to discourage Taiwan's independence by decreasing both the quantity and the quality of arms sales to Taiwan.

8. The United States should openly declare that Taiwan will not have access to theater missile defense (TMD). Soon after President Clinton's visit to China in the summer of 1998, there were talks both in the United States and in Taiwan about including Taiwan in TMD. Such talks encouraged the trend toward Taiwan's independence and harmed the atmosphere for cross-strait relations. In an April 1999 discussion regarding TMD, Senator Kay Bailey Hutchison made her position on TMD clear. She said that TMD is to protect U.S. soldiers in East Asia, not to protect Japan, South Korea, or Taiwan. TMD would remain in U.S. hands and not be transferred to other countries. The U.S. government should make a similar public announcement.

9. The United States should clarify its commitment to "not support Taiwan independence." During the past few years U.S. officials, including President Clinton, have reiterated this principle. Yet it remains abstract and vague. Some U.S. scholars, such as Joseph Nye, advocate more concrete measures, suggesting that the United States make clear that, if Taiwan declares independence, the United States will not recognize it, will not cooperate with Taiwan in defense, and

will discourage the international community from recognizing it. The effects of such measures to discourage Taiwan's independence are obvious. The U.S. government should make such an announcement.

10. The United States should clarify its principle of non-use of force in solving the Taiwan issue. In discussions about such questions in the autumn of 1996, Kenneth Lieberthal said that "the United States would most likely become involved in the issue militarily if the mainland uses force without a serious provocation from Taiwan." When asked "What do you mean by serious provocation?" he said, "for instance, if Taiwan declares independence." He did not think that the United States would intervene militarily if the mainland used force because Taiwan had declared independence. Asked the same question again after he joined the White House in the summer of 1998, Lieberthal replied, "Since I have now become an official it's better to forget everything I said before." But it is important for the United States to make its non-use of force principle conditional rather that unconditional as it is now. This would better serve the interests on both sides of the strait as well as U.S. interests.

PART TWO

———————

"ONE CHINA" AND
INTERNATIONAL SPACE

CHAPTER THREE

THE GORDIAN KNOT IN CROSS-STRAIT RELATIONS: THE QUESTION OF TAIWAN'S PARTICIPATION IN INTERNATIONAL ORGANIZATIONS
Loh I-cheng

LOOKING DOWN THE ROAD, one sees few grounds for optimism as far as cross-strait relations at the turn of the century are concerned. A great deal depends on the outcome of the Republic of China's (ROC's) presidential election in March 2000. Even if the winner of the five-way race is more acceptable to Beijing than the incumbent, there seems little chance the People's Republic of China (PRC) could or would change its long-standing and thus far successful policy of diplomatically isolating Taipei.

But, as seen from the other side of the glass partition, that policy of denying the ROC *lebensraum* in the international arena may achieve exactly the opposite of the PRC's declared objective of eventual unification of the two Chinas.

Taiwan has become a veritable democracy, on that point there is no argument. Even Beijing's propaganda machines on the mainland and in Hong Kong have steered clear of it as an issue. It follows that any serious attempt to win over Taiwan, without reducing the island to rubble, must take into consideration the attitude, perhaps allegiance is a better word, of its 22 million inhabitants.

NEW RED FLAG

Everyone can understand the PRC's position. Never mind that there are 64 officially recognized nationalities on the mainland. Never mind that, in 3,000 years of recorded history, the periods when what geographically constitutes China today was divided into more than one entity were almost as long as the periods China was united under one government. To the Chinese, rightly or wrongly, China is one nation.

Nobody truly believes in communism any more. China's economy faces the double challenge of massive unemployment and deflation. The government feels so insecure that it banned the practice of *falun gong*, a form of calisthenics combined with harmless mysticism. Thus it is understandable that the PRC needs a new ideology to rally its 1.2 billion people.

Consider Beijing's staged, angry reaction to the bombing of its embassy in Belgrade, its increasingly closer relationship with Russia symbolized by President Jiang's hurried meeting with Boris Yeltsin in November 1998, and the so-far muted but unmistakable anti-U.S. rumblings within China's ruling circle since the beginning of 1999. All manifest a shifting emphasis that suits the policy needs at present and will remain the ideological anchor in the foreseeable future.

Not that it has not been there before, but there has been less emphasis on it since the early days of the Sino-Japanese war that began in 1937. It was certainly absent during the early 1950s when Mao was enjoying his honeymoon with Stalin. It gradually came to the fore during almost three decades of the Sino-Soviet split. It faded again somewhat when Deng Xiaoping opened China to the irresistible tide of modernization. Now it again becomes the red flag held high in China. That policy, that new religion, is Chinese nationalism.

The power of nationalism is so strong that not only the ruling elite, but also the majority of the Chinese people, honestly believe it their sacred duty to bring Taiwan back into the motherland's outstretched arms. Theoretically, there are military, economic, or diplomatic means to achieve this policy goal. But pragmatically, there are few choices.

LIMITED OPTIONS

Take the military option, for example. The March 1996 missile crisis made it clear to the Chinese Communist Party Politburo that listening to the hawks among its ranks would bring their country only into direct confrontation with the world's sole superpower. For political reasons, Beijing could not consent to renouncing the use of force in cross-strait relations, lest it encourage the movement for independence in Taiwan.

This dilemma almost gave Beijing schizophrenia. The frustrated PRC was furious with President Lee's "special state-to-state relationship" remark. During July and August 1999, the only outlet for its anger was to allow the media in Hong Kong under its control to put banner headlines on their front pages each day, darkly prophesying that a naval blockade or direct assault against Taiwan or some outlying islands was imminent. The huffing and puffing suited the bears at the Taipei Stock Exchange who used the war scare to fleece panicking small investors, but the market soon returned to normal. Life for the majority of people on Taiwan went on merrily as before. Such crying-wolf tactics probably will not work the next time around.

The economic option also smacks of a paper tiger without teeth. In spite of the ballyhoo about China becoming the world's largest economy sometime in the first decade of the twenty-first century, tiny Taiwan stubbornly stays in the race for economic growth in Asia, refusing to wither or just go away. It is embarrassing to Beijing that in matters of trade and economic development, the PRC seems to need Taiwan more than the other way around.

The "three links" is not just a slogan for reunification. Taiwan's allowing direct trade, postal and telecom service, and air and sea transport between the two shores would cut business costs significantly and serve the economic interest of the PRC. Thus, although it takes only one directive from Beijing to kick out of the mainland the 43,000 Taiwanese businesses, such a step would hurt Beijing more than Taipei.

No wonder, in spite of unprecedented tension across the strait in recent months, Beijing keeps reassuring those investors that they will be protected. To soothe Taiwanese businesspeople, the PRC announced that it would publish soon the implementation regulations of the "Law for Protection of Investment by Compatriots from Taiwan," long promised but still delayed.

ONLY WEAPON LEFT

That leaves only the diplomatic field where the PRC wields great influence both as a permanent member of the United Nations Security Council and as an emerging major power not only in Asia but also in the world. Employing every means at their disposal, Beijing's diplomats have deftly persuaded or ruthlessly pressured most countries of the world, plus all international organizations affiliated with the UN, into accepting their dictum: "There is only one China, and Taiwan is part of China." Except for a few special cases such as the Olympics, the Asian Development Bank, APEC (the Asia-Pacific Economic Cooperation), and the World Trade Organization (WTO), the PRC's boycott of Taipei is almost complete.

As a result, Taiwan has suffered humiliation and defeat in the international arena at almost every turn since 1971, when it was booted out of the UN. Those unfamiliar with the issue have often questioned why Taiwan does not accept the one-country, two-systems deal offered by China. Beijing has promised that Taiwan could keep intact its own political, economic, and social system for 50 years, that no troops or officials would be sent there from Beijing, and that someone from Taiwan could even become vice president of the central government.

Until now, Taipei's standard answer has been that one country, two systems is unacceptable because Hong Kong and Macao were western colonies left from the nineteenth century. They are not comparable with Taiwan. That kind of statement may be sufficient for the man on the street, but it runs the risk of being a non sequitur in more discriminating discussions.

The real impediment in today's difficult atmosphere is that each side lacks confidence in the other's actions or promises. From Taipei's point of view, there is nothing in one country, two systems that Taiwan does not already enjoy as an independent state, whether or not other countries so recognize it.

There is also a catch-22 between the lines: The promise that Taiwan can keep its own armed forces becomes meaningless when only Beijing can handle matters relating to defense and foreign affairs. The shrill voice emanating from across the strait objecting to theater missile defense only reinforces that nagging suspicion instead of diminishing it.

To the people on Taiwan, accepting one country, two systems simply means trading the security guarantee of the Taiwan Relations Act, however vague or imprecise, for the mercy of the communist regime in Beijing. It would be nothing short of abject surrender. Why such a perception exists should not be difficult for the think tanks or senior officials of the PRC to understand, yet they are either unwilling or unable to come up with an alternative offer.

SKIRMISHES AT THE UN

Today's instant news reports carry information to every corner of the globe, yet there are the same mistakes, albeit for different reasons, of nineteenth century journalism, namely, the need to simplify stories to save telegraph charges. A ready example is the reporting of Taiwan's knocking at the UN door, which all media without exception have characterized throughout the past eight years as an effort "to rejoin the United Nations."

In cross-strait discussions, the ROC never really challenged Beijing's sovereignty claim, asking only that it be laid aside until conditions are ripe for unification. At the UN, there are ample precedents of one sovereign nation with several votes. The former Soviet Union had three votes. Both East and West Germany were UN members, but that did not hinder their unification. North and South Korea still sit in the same General Assembly Hall. The PRC maintained diplomatic relations with both Germanys and does so with both Koreas, yet threatens dire consequences should any country adopt the same policy toward the two Chinas.

Taipei's timid efforts began in 1992, the year following the election of Lee Teng-hui in his own right to the first term of his presidency and his unilateral termination of the status of civil war between the two sides of the Taiwan Strait. From the beginning, Taiwan made clear that in appealing to the UN, it was not challenging the PRC's position or membership in any way. It carefully avoided the use of such words as "rejoin" or "return" to the body. It merely appealed for the right to "participate" in its activities in whatever manner the membership saw fit.

In 1993, it made another concession, asking only that a special "study committee" be established to review the situation in accordance with the universality principle of the charter and precedents set by divided countries in the UN. Even such a watered down proposal was shut out by the UN General Assembly's General Committee for the next four years.

Only in 1997 did the sponsoring friends of the ROC become so disgusted as to urge the UN General Assembly to review GA resolution 2758 (XXVI) of October 25, 1971, "owing to the fundamental change in the international situation and to the coexistence of two governments across the Taiwan Strait." While it is certain that this draft resolution will be defeated again in 1999, the ROC will cheerfully propose it again next year because it has no other choice. The joke in Taipei is that it took the PRC 22 years to join the UN, so Taiwan still has 14 more years to go in this marathon race.

BATTLE OF COMMAS

Over the years, PRC pressure has been so pervasive that, as far as the United Nations is concerned, Taiwan just does not exist. Although the ROC is 25th in per capita income, 14th among trading nations of the world, and 7th of capital-exporting countries, nowhere in the *UN Statistical Yearbook*, that all-important reference volume, can one find mention of Taiwan.

Fortunately for us, there have been exceptions in the UN's behavioral pattern. The ROC currently sits in such diverse organizations as the International Olympics Committee, the Asian Development Bank, and APEC in addition to 14 other intergovernmental organizations and 955 international bodies that are nongovernmental in nature. The ROC also participates as an observer in many other international organizations, notably the WTO.

In such bodies as the Central American Bank of Economic Integration, the Asian Productivity Organization, and the Asian Vegetable Research and Development Center, no one questioned the use of the official name as the Republic of China. When participating in APEC itself or its myriad groupings, or competing in sporting events from the Asian Games to the Olympics, the country becomes "Chinese Taipei." In still others, simply "Taiwan" or "China (Taiwan)" are used for pragmatic reasons.

Nowhere was this pragmatism more apparent than at the WTO, where choice of the cumbersome title of a separate "customs area of Taiwan, Penghu, Kinmen, and Matsu" avoided objection from the PRC. This flexibility reminds one of President Lee's comment when he first visited Singapore where the local media referred to him as "President Lee Teng-hui **from** Taiwan" and not "**of** Taiwan." On his return to Taipei, when domestic media asked him what he thought of the title, he replied that it was "not satisfactory," but "acceptable."

The ROC cannot accept any inference that Taiwan is merely a province of the PRC, thus subjugated to Beijing's "central government." Taipei has indicated that it could live with "China (Taipei)" or "China (Taiwan)" since these terms reflect the situation on the ground. It would even accept "Taipei China" without a comma, in which Taipei is an adjective. But it draws the line at "Taipei, China," because the inference is that Taipei is part of the PRC in the same way as Hong Kong, China or Shanghai, China is.

Battling over a comma seems laughable to outsiders. To Chinese on both sides of the Taiwan Strait, it is part of the tug of war, a psychological battle that will not soon end.

LEE'S BOMBSHELL

Rightly or wrongly, President Lee has the reputation of shooting from the hip when asked a loaded question. More than once in the past, subordinates have scrambled to mop up for him in ways not so different from a White House spokesman trying to "clarify" something a U.S. president has said.

But what happened on July 9, 1999, was not one of those occasions. On that day Lee was interviewed by Deutsche Welle (Voice of Germany). Although Dieter Weirich, president of the German radio network, nominally headed the news team, the difficult questions were asked by Günter Knabe, its seasoned Asian bureau chief, stationed in Hong Kong.

After the usual compliments on Taiwan's economic miracle and democratization, Knabe asked Lee: "Taiwan is considered by Beijing's government as a 'renegade province'. This is a cause for permanent tensions and threats against your island from the mainland. How do you cope with these dangers?"

According to the transcript released later, Lee replied:

> I will answer your question from the historical and legal viewpoints. There has been an impasse in cross-strait relations because the Beijing authorities ignore the very fact that the two sides are two different jurisdictions and that the Chinese mainland continues to pose a military threat against us. The historical fact is that since the establishment of the Chinese Communist regime in 1949, it has never ruled the territories under the Republic of China's jurisdiction: Taiwan, Penghu, Kinmen and Matsu.

He continued:

> In the 1991 Constitutional Amendment, Article 10 of the Additional Articles (now Article 11) limits the area covered by the Constitution to that of the Taiwan area, and recognizes the legitimacy of the rule of the People's Republic of China on the Chinese mainland. Articles 1 and 4 of the Additional Articles clearly stipulate that the members of the Legislative Yuan and the National Assembly shall be elected from the Taiwan area only.

> The 1992 Constitutional Amendments further stipulate in Article 2 of the Additional Articles that the president and the vice president shall be popularly elected by the people of the Taiwan area. Thus, the reconfigured national agencies represent only the people of the Taiwan area. The legitimacy of the rule of the country comes from the mandate of the Taiwan people, and has nothing to do with the people on the mainland.

The 1991 Constitutional Amendments have placed cross-strait relations as a state-to-state relationship or at least a special state-to-state relationship, rather than an internal relationship between a legitimate government and a renegade group, or between a central government and a local government. Thus, the Beijing authorities' characterization of Taiwan as a "renegade province" is historically and legally untrue.

The extremely competitive media in Taiwan seized on that one sentence from a rambling discourse and came out with headlines screaming "President Outlines Two-States Theory." As expected, pandemonium broke loose.

DIVERSE REACTIONS

Reactions to such sensational reporting came as swiftly as thunder and summer rain. In retrospect, it is difficult to say who is to blame. Beijing became livid with rage, because the headline-grabbing Taiwanese media simplified several paragraphs of dialectics into three little words, *liang guo lun* (two-state theory), leaving its explanation to the reader's imagination.

The PRC had long suspected that Lee was a wolf in sheep's clothing, hiding pro-independence leanings under the cloak of his KMT (Kuomintang) chairmanship. This latest episode only exposed Lee's true colors, Beijing's mouthpieces charged. Gleeful PLA (People's Liberation Army) generals agitated for renewing missile tests offshore "to teach Taiwan a lesson," but cooler heads in the Politburo again prevailed.

The Association for Relations Across the Taiwan Strait (ARATS) at first hoped that Koo Chen-fu, the wise elder statesman, might somehow repair the damage. When that hope dimmed, Beijing announced that Wang Daohan would postpone his scheduled autumn 1999 visit to Taiwan "until a more opportune moment," meaning after March 2000 when Taiwan's election results are known.

The PLA still held military maneuvers in August 1999 to appease the generals. But the amphibious landing exercises took place near

Hainan, and the missile test was conducted far inland in the northwest to show Washington and the world that the PRC can be reasonable even though provoked by troublemaker Lee. Not until early September 1999 did the Nanjing and Guangzhou Military Regions hold large-scale maneuvers, aiming more to put psychological pressure on the autumn APEC meeting than to intimidate Taiwan.

For its part, Washington was upset at first, assuming that Lee made his highly provocative gesture to exploit the near-freezing temperature in U.S.-PRC relations following the Belgrade bombing incident and breakdown in WTO talks. According to a White House spokesman, Lee's idea runs directly contrary to Washington's one-China policy, a pillar of U.S. foreign policy in the region.

The State Department also expressed displeasure that Taipei failed to consult Washington before such an important shift of position and suspected it might have been designed to aid the campaign of Vice President Lien Chan, who was feeling pressure from rival James Soong.

Although there are five presidential candidates in Taiwan, the strongest challenge to Lien came not from the opposition Democratic Progressive Party's (DPP's) Chen Shui-bian, ex-mayor of Taipei, but from Georgetown-educated Soong, ex-governor of Taiwan and former KMT secretary general. Soong, who consistently leads all others in pre-election polls, has been expelled from the KMT for breaching party discipline in running as an independent candidate.

Curiously, no one in Washington paused to consider that the surprise sprung by President Lee could have an entirely different purpose, namely, that he was seriously preparing for cross-strait political negotiations. For more than a year, the United States had been urging both Chinas to hold talks aimed at reducing tension in the Taiwan Strait, with special emphasis on the planned visit of Wang Daohan to Taiwan in the autumn of 1999.

Scholars, journalists, and officials alike in Taiwan studied with microscopes statements and even impromptu responses to questions by middle-level U.S. officials this year and last that advocated "interim agreements." There was even a spirited debate on whether the word "agreement" was singular or plural when pronounced by U.S. officials such as Stanley Roth or Ken Lieberthal.

OPINION POLLS

President Lee insisted that he did not use the phrase "a special state-to-state relationship" on the spur of the moment. It had been under study for more than a year, he said, and the occasion presented itself when Deutsche Welle requested an interview, given the history of German unification after 45 years of separate statehood. He wanted to emphasize, he later told overseas Chinese delegates, that both sides of the Taiwan Strait must be placed on equal footing if they are to negotiate their differences seriously.

But even he did not count on the cacophony of domestic and foreign criticism following July 9. The other opposition group, the New Party, immediately accused Lee of treason and demanded his resignation. Most radio and television talk shows and call-in programs, reflecting negative media reports from mainland China and the United States, lambasted him mercilessly. The DPP partly agreed but with reservations. The only exception was the Taiwan Independence Party (*jian guo tang*), which lamented that Lee did not go far enough.

Government officials at first scrambled to cover for him; some went further than others. The dust gradually settled when, to most people's surprise, all opinion polls showed that a majority of the responding public agreed with the essence of President Lee's latest statement, if not the words or the way he expressed it.

Polls have come of age in Taiwan and are regarded as generally reliable in measuring public opinion on specific issues. In this case, perhaps most revealing is the *United Daily News* poll, taken on a continuing basis to gauge what the public thinks in line with breaking news. This newspaper, which has remained highly critical of Lee for all 10 years of his presidency and has frequently received his wrath, conducted three consecutive surveys (see Table 3.1) of public reaction to Lee's statement in the two weeks following that bombshell:

Table 3.1
Poll on Lee's Statement of a "Special State-to-State Relationship,"
July 1999

Dates	Number of Samples	Agree (%)	Disagree (%)	Don't Know (%)
July 10-11	1,012	48.9	29.6	21.6
July 15	843	45.9	26.5	27.6
July 23-24	995	55.8	24.1	20.1

These polls showed that immediately after the first news, approximately 50 percent of the respondents agreed with the president, almost 30 percent disagreed, and 20 percent had no opinion. After the spate of criticism from the PRC and the United States, the number of "don't knows" went up sharply, while those who agreed and those who disagreed decreased by almost the same margin. Finally, when the matter was thoroughly aired and people had time to think, those who agreed went up by almost 7 percent at the expense of the other two columns.

There were also polls with comparable results by organizations ranging from other media to political parties, although the percentages of those who agreed were somewhat higher than those reported by the *United Daily News*. Worth mentioning is a poll of 587 business leaders by the *Commerce Weekly* on July 19–20, 1999. It showed 78.4 percent in agreement, only 15.3 percent in disagreement, and 6.3 percent undecided, evidence that businesspeople overwhelmingly support a clear-cut position for Taiwan when negotiation starts with the mainland.

Whether the message from these polls caught the PRC's eye is not known. Media reports from Beijing indicated that no drastic action was contemplated if *liang guo lun* were not written into the ROC constitution or the *Guidelines for National Unification*, the official policy document adopted in 1991 that set the ultimate goal as "unification of China." In short, Beijing realized it could not really use force if Taiwan demonstrates, not by word but by deed, that it has no intention of unilaterally declaring independence.

The ROC responded accordingly. The second conference of the 15th KMT Congress, August 28–29, 1999, in Taipei, endorsed *liang guo lun* in a resolution but made clear that Taiwan will not give up its constitution or its goal of national unification. The usually irrepressible Lee, in another off-the-cuff comment before that time, had blurted, "Let the arguments rage, the louder the better, so that more people in the world will notice the existence of the Republic of China." This comment was largely ignored outside Taiwan.

DIPLOMATIC CEASE-FIRE?

Friends point out that the word *lebensraum* at the beginning of this article smacks too much of Hitlerism and German aggression. Yes, but *living space* is more emphatic than *breathing space*, which is too weak to convey an intended urgency.

Whatever his faults, one must concede that President Lee does have the uncanny knack of putting his finger on the pulse of public sentiment in Taiwan. Nobody can deny that, for a thousand different reasons, the feeling of the people on Taiwan toward their compatriots on the mainland has undergone a sea change in the past decade. Any objective assessment will find that most of the warmth and goodwill the people on Taiwan felt in 1989 toward mainland China have now disappeared.

The China Credit Information Service (CCIS), contracted by the Mainland Affairs Council, conducted a telephone poll of 1,067 persons August 27–31, 1999, with a margin of error of +/-3 percent. The CCIS, similar to Dow Jones in the United States, enjoys a solid reputation in market research and measurement. The survey was scientifically done to conform with the population profile of the country. Noteworthy findings included the following:

- 66.7 percent regard the PRC as either "unfriendly" or "very unfriendly" toward the people on Taiwan. Only 27.3 percent chose "friendly" or "very friendly." When the question is slightly changed to ask what they think the attitude of the PRC government toward the ROC government is, the total of "unfriendly" and "very unfriendly" responses rose to 88.5 percent; those who saw it as "friendly" and "very friendly" dropped to 8.4 percent.

- 85.9 percent either "disagree" or "strongly disagree" with the PRC's one-China definition. In addition, 91.1 percent either "agree" or "strongly agree" with the statement that the ROC is an independent, sovereign state.

- 65.5 percent either "agree" or "strongly agree" with what President Lee said about the cross-strait relationship, that is, "a special state-to-state relationship." Only 24.8 percent either "disagree" or "strongly disagree."

- When asked: "If developing diplomatic relations with other countries will create tensions in cross-strait relations, do you still support the continuation of such efforts?" 79.4 percent replied that they still "support" or "strongly support." Only 17.7 percent said they would not support or would be very much against developing such relations.

Because of the timely value of the CCIS survey, the original questionnaire and detailed results are included.

The alarm bell sounded by this poll was that, for the first time in history, those who would choose independence, immediately or after a suitable interval, reached 28.1 percent. Given six choices, 12.2 percent prefer not to take sides and maintain the status quo permanently, 39.6 percent would keep the status quo and see which way the wind blows, and only 18.7 percent would choose immediate unification, or the status quo now and unification later. That last statistic was also the lowest ever recorded.

Without doubt, this alarming trend of public sentiment in Taiwan can be traced directly to the PRC's one-China dictum and its inflexible attitude toward the legitimate aspirations for some diplomatic elbow room on the part of the people of Taiwan. The behavior of President Jiang Zemin and Foreign Minister Tang Jiaxuan at the APEC summit in Auckland showed that the PRC leadership believed they were ahead in the game of pressuring Washington to force Taipei to give in to its demands.

The White House is unlikely to oblige all the way. On the one hand, the "tilting" of U.S. policy that has been self-evident in the past few years may continue to favor the PRC. On the other hand, the people of Taiwan genuinely believe they are being pushed to the wall by Beijing's dogmatic and unreasonable attitude. That is the reason for the pessimism expressed above.

At the root, diplomatic pressure alone cannot win the battle for Beijing. An honest assessment would be that cross-strait relations are likely to remain where they are well into the first decade of the twenty-first century. The ROC may not get far in its quest for international space, but the PRC will not be able to strip Taiwan of all its staunch friends, with or without diplomatic relations. The result will be a total deadlock, while disappointment grows into hatred and brothers become enemies.

If worse comes to worst, and that is unthinkable, a variation of the situation in East Timor cannot be ruled out. President Clinton alluded to it in Auckland: "[there is] the proposition that these people have too much at stake in a peaceful future, benefiting all their children, to let the present difficulties deteriorate into a confrontation in which, in the end, all would suffer." One can have full confidence that cross-strait relations will not reach such a stage, but the key is in the PRC's hands.

Is there a way out of this impasse? Only if a miracle happens; for example, a diplomatic cease-fire is agreed on when Wang Daohan visits Taiwan next spring. The arrangement could be that both sides pledge not to raid the other's camp of countries with which it has formal relations. Let the ROC keep its current 28, while the PRC has its 153 or more. The ROC should be allowed to participate fully in international organizations under the premise that its role in no way affects the single sovereignty and territorial integrity of China as a whole. The examples of the Germanys and the Koreas should be sufficient for other countries to readily accept, and even embrace, the idea.

In September 1990, the prime ministers of North and South Korea met in Seoul to talk about reunification in a dazzling display of bold initiative and attractive slogans. The DPRK (Democratic People's

Republic of Korea) demanded everything and gave nothing in return. Today most people have forgotten that meeting, except for those in Taiwan who paid close attention to the reason it failed. The ROC is carefully preparing for the second Koo-Wang talks, on every political subject, with sincerity and genuine desire for peace in the region.

There is a Chinese saying: *tui yi bu hai kuo tian kung*, "take one step backward, and you will find that the sky and the sea are so much wider." One can only pray that President Jiang or someone else in Beijing will cut this Gordian knot that inextricably ties cross-strait relations to public sentiment in Taiwan and save the Chinese nation from a prolonged period of forced separation.

PUBLIC OPINION SURVEY: QUESTIONNAIRE ON CURRENT STATUS OF CROSS-STRAIT RELATIONS

Conducted by the China Credit Information Service under Contract to the Mainland Affairs Council
August 27–31, 1999

How do you do, sir (madam)? I am an interviewer of the China Credit Information Service. We are doing a public opinion survey of how people see the current state of cross-strait relations. May I have a few minutes of your time to ask a few questions? Thank you very much.

First, we'd like to know what you think of President Lee's recent views on cross-strait relations.

(1) President Lee recently said that the relationship between Taiwan and the mainland is a kind of "special state-to-state relationship." Are you aware of that?

91.3%	•	Yes
8.7%	•	No

(2) Regarding this view that "the relationship between Taiwan and the mainland is a kind of special state-to-state relationship," do you agree or disagree?

22.3%	•	1	Strongly agree
43.2%	•	2	Agree
20.1%	•	3	Disagree
4.7%	•	4	Strongly disagree
9.7%	•	5	Don't know/No opinion

(3) The mainland has said that, because President Lee describes our relations with the mainland as a special state-to-state relationship, the basis for continued dialogue between the Straits Exchange Foundation (SEF) and the Association for Relations Across the Taiwan Strait (ARATS) no longer exists. Do you agree or disagree with this view on the part of the mainland?

2.6%	•	1	Strongly agree
19.1%	•	2	Agree
49.5%	•	3	Disagree
17.4%	•	4	Strongly disagree
11.3%	•	5	Don't know/No opinion

(4) The mainland says: "Taiwan is a part of China, and the People's Republic of China is the only legitimate representative of all China." Do you agree or disagree with this saying?

1.3%	•	1	Strongly agree
10.6%	•	2	Agree
45.4%	•	3	Disagree
40.5%	•	4	Strongly disagree
2.2%	•	5	Don't know/No opinion

(5) Do you agree with the saying that "the Republic of China is an independent, sovereign state"?

51.1%	•	1	Strongly agree
40.1%	•	2	Agree
5.8%	•	3	Disagree
0.9%	•	4	Strongly disagree
2.1%	•	5	Don't know/No opinion

Continuing, may I ask you for your opinions about cross-strait exchanges and future relations:

(6) Do you regard the mainland government's attitude toward our government as friendly (good) or unfriendly (bad)?

0.6%	•	1	Very friendly
7.8%	•	2	Friendly
52.8%	•	3	Unfriendly
35.7%	•	4	Very unfriendly
3.2%	•	5	Don't know/No opinion

(7) Do you regard the mainland government's attitude toward the people of Taiwan as friendly (good) or unfriendly (bad)?

1.2%	•	1	Very friendly
26.1%	•	2	Friendly
48.5%	•	3	Unfriendly
18.2%	•	4	Very unfriendly
6.0%	•	5	Don't know/No opinion

(8) In recent years, our government has gradually opened up private sector exchanges with the mainland. Do you think the speed of such private sector exchanges are too fast, too slow, or just right?

23.5%	•	1	Too fast
18.0%	•	2	Too slow
49.4%	•	3	Just right
9.1%	•	4	Don't know/No opinion

(9) Regarding Taiwan's relationship with the mainland, there are these different points of view: (1) Unification as soon as possible; (2) Declaring independence as soon as possible; (3) Maintaining the status quo, with unification in the future; (4) Maintaining the status quo, with independence in the future; (5) Maintaining the status quo, postponing the decision for unification or independence, depending on future situation; and (6) Permanently maintaining the status quo. Would you tell me which one of these options you prefer?

2.4%	•	1	Unification as soon as possible
14.3%	•	2	Independence as soon as possible
16.3%	•	3	Maintaining the status quo, with unification in the future
13.8%	•	4	Maintaining the status quo, with independence in the future
39.6%	•	5	Maintaining the status quo, postponing the decision until situation clears up
12.2%	•	6	Maintaining the status quo forever
1.3%	•	7	Don't know/No opinion

(10) Regarding future development of cross-strait relations, the mainland's doctrine of "one China" regards Taiwan as a local government under its rule, and the government of the Republic of China will no longer exist. Do you agree or disagree with their position?

2.8%	•	1	Strongly agree
7.6%	•	2	Agree
42.7%	•	3	Disagree
44.5%	•	4	Strongly disagree
2.3%	•	5	Don't know/No opinion

(11) Some people believe that it is more important to develop Taiwan's relationship with the mainland, and there are others who believe that it is more important to develop a relationship with other countries. Which one of these do you regard as more important than the other?

20.1%	•	1	Develop relationship with the mainland
31.3%	•	2	Develop relationships with other countries
46.1%	•	3	Both are equally important
2.4%	•	4	Don't know/No opinion

(12) If developing diplomatic relations with other countries will create tensions between the two sides of the Taiwan Strait, do you still support the continuation of such efforts?

23.8%	•	1	Strongly support
55.6%	•	2	Support
15.6%	•	3	Will not support
2.1%	•	4	Will strongly not support
2.0%	•	5	Don't know/No opinion

(13) Some people advocate that only when the political system and way of life on both sides of the Taiwan Strait are close enough, then both sides can start talking about unification. Some people support this idea and others oppose it. What is your opinion?

18.5%	•	1	Strongly support
48.0%	•	2	Support
20.7%	•	3	Do not support
6.9%	•	4	Strongly do not support
5.9%	•	5	Don't know/No opinion

(14) Some people say that we must seek equality between both sides, then and only then would it be helpful for our government to negotiate with the mainland. Do you agree or disagree with this view?

34.0%	•	1	Strongly agree
50.0%	•	2	Agree
10.6%	•	3	Disagree
2.5%	•	4	Strongly disagree
2.8%	•	5	Don't know/No opinion

(15) Our government insists that official contacts and negotiations by and between Taiwan and the mainland should be based on an equal status. Do you think it is necessary for our government to insist on this principle?

48.5%	•	1	Very necessary
37.0%	•	2	Necessary
9.5%	•	3	Unnecessary
2.2%	•	4	Very unnecessary
2.7%	•	5	Don't know/No opinion

Finally, allow me to ask you some questions relating to the visit here by the president of the Association for Relations Across the Taiwan Strait (ARATS).

(16) Mr. Wang Daohan, president of ARATS of the mainland, is scheduled to visit Taiwan this fall. Do you welcome the visit by Mr. Wang?

27.1%	•	1	Very welcome
59.8%	•	2	Welcome
5.2%	•	3	Not welcome
2.1%	•	4	Strongly not welcome
5.9%	•	5	Don't know/No opinion

(17) If Mr. Wang is to postpone his visit, do you still welcome him to Taiwan at an opportune moment?

22.3%	•	1	Very welcome
62.8%	•	2	Welcome
6.8%	•	3	Not welcome
2.2%	•	4	Strongly not welcome
5.9%	•	5	Don't know/No opinion

(18) The mainland indicated that Taiwan must first withdraw the "special state-to-state relationship" theory before it would agree for Mr. Wang to visit Taiwan. Do you think this demand is reasonable?

1.9%	•	1	Very reasonable
11.8%	•	2	Reasonable
5.4%	•	3	Unreasonable
34.9%	•	4	Very unreasonable
6.1%	•	5	Don't know/No opinion

(19) If Mr. Wang comes on a visit, do you think it would be helpful for the development of cross-strait relations?

10.7%	•	1	Very helpful
57.9%	•	2	Helpful
20.2%	•	3	Unhelpful
4.3%	•	4	Very unhelpful
6.8%	•	5	Don't know/No opinion

BASIC INFORMATION ABOUT RESPONDENTS

(1) **Please tell me your sex.**

50.5%	•	1	Male
49.5%	•	2	Female

(2) **Please tell me your age.**

27.0%	•	1	20–29 years
28.4%	•	2	30–39 years
23.1%	•	3	40–49 years
12.1%	•	4	50–59 years
9.5%	•	5	60–69 years

(3) **What is your education?**

15.5%	•	1	Grade school or less
10.7%	•	2	Junior high
31.7%	•	3	Senior high
20.7%	•	4	Junior college
18.3%	•	5	University
3.2%	•	6	Graduate school or higher

(4) **Can you tell us your profession (for retired persons, ask for his or her profession before retirement)?**

13.5%	•	1	Public service (including military and teaching)
32.1%	•	2	Commercial sector (including service sector)
17.7%	•	3	Industrial sector
5.6%	•	4	Free profession
18.2%	•	5	Housekeeping
7.7%	•	6	Student
2.9%	•	7	Agricultural sector
2.3%	•	8	Others (please specify)

(5) Of which one of the following political parties do you consider yourself a supporter?

18.2%	•	1	KMT (Kuomintang)
10.8%	•	2	DPP (Democratic Progressive Party)
1.5%	•	3	New Party
0.0%	•	4	Taiwan Independence Party (jian guo tang)
69.4%	•	5	No particular party affiliation
0.2%	•	6	Other party (please specify)

(6) Can you tell us your native place (ji guan)?

10.9%	•	1	Native born, hakka speaking
75.1%	•	2	Native born, minnan (southern Fujian) speaking
12.8%	•	3	Various provinces of the mainland
1.1%	•	4	Original inhabitant (aborigines)
0.1%	•	5	Others (please specify)

(7) In our society, some call themselves Taiwanese, some call themselves Chinese. And some say they are both. What do you see yourself as?

44.8%	•	1	Taiwanese
13.1%	•	2	Chinese
39.9%	•	3	Both
2.2%	•	4	Don't know/No opinion

(8) **In which part of Taiwan do you live?**

42.7%	•	1	Northern Taiwan
22.6%	•	2	Central Taiwan
29.2%	•	3	Southern Taiwan
5.4%	•	4	Eastern Taiwan

(9) **How many times have you visited the mainland within the past ten years?**

75.2%	•	1	None
11.2%	•	2	Once
7.6%	•	3	2 to 4 times
6.0%	•	4	5 times or more

(10) **Do you or any member of your family have investments on the mainland or are you doing business there?**

| 18.5% | • | 1 | Yes |
| 81.5% | • | 2 | No |

(11) **Are you or any member of your family attending school or working (employed) on the mainland?**

| 10.3% | • | 1 | Yes |
| 89.7% | • | 2 | No |

Telephone No. _____

Name of Respondent _____

Our interview has come to an end. Thank you very much.

CHAPTER FOUR

INTERNATIONAL SPACE FOR WHAT? BEIJING'S CONCERNS AND POSITION REGARDING TAIWAN'S PARTICIPATION IN INTERNATIONAL ORGANIZATIONS

Chu Shulong

TAIWAN'S BID FOR INTERNATIONAL SPACE, sometimes called its pragmatic diplomacy, has been a major area of confrontation between mainland China and Taiwan. Beijing suspects that Taiwan's international bid is for independence; Beijing thus cannot tolerate Taiwan's efforts to expand its international space. In Taiwan, a strong majority support Taipei's effort to enlarge international space, even if it causes friction between the mainland and Taiwan. Indeed, a great number of people in Taiwan consider international space more important than cross-strait relations. The dilemma is real and fundamental: The two sides across the strait have fought over the issue for many years, expending significant resources, including money and energy.

BEIJING'S CONCERN

Beijing understands that people in Taiwan need to go abroad to do business, study, travel, and visit family members and relatives. Beijing does not oppose these activities. To facilitate economic and cultural activities, Beijing understands that arrangements are needed between Taiwan and other countries and regions around the world. Beijing does not oppose these efforts, considering that such activities and arrangements can and should occur within the boundary of the economic and culture arenas. In contrast, Beijing opposes anything that goes beyond economic and cultural arenas and business and personal needs. Therefore, in every major bilateral and multilateral agreement that the PRC signs with foreign governments and international organizations, including cultural and sports organizations, Beijing sets a clear boundary on Taiwan's international activities, including names and flags.

Beijing worries that Taiwan wants to go beyond its international boundary. In the past 10 years under Lee Teng-hui, Taipei has tried hard to go beyond the boundary. This forces Beijing to consider what Taipei really wants. In the past 10 years, Beijing has consistently criticized Taipei's international bid for independence, although Taipei has consistently denied that such is its purpose. Lee Teng-hui's two-state-theory statement on July 9, 1999, clearly showed that Beijing's concerns are correct. Taipei's bid for greater international space is not only for doing business abroad and tourism but also for advancing a two-state relationship between the mainland and Taiwan.

Many people in Taiwan argue that the PRC's position regarding Taiwan's international status indicates that Beijing does not respect their human rights or understand that public opinion in Taiwan indicates a desire for more international space. This argument does not hold water for two reasons. First, Beijing understands and respects the rights of people in Taiwan to travel and do business abroad. Actually almost all people in Taiwan enjoy these rights; they can go anywhere they want. Only Lee Teng-hui and a handful of Taiwan's high-level officials do not have the freedom to go where they want. Second, Beijing understands and respects the opinion of 21 million people living in Taiwan, but it also has to understand and respect the opinion of 1.2 billion people living on the mainland. When public opinion on Taiwan and the mainland conflict, Beijing must stand on the mainland's side, just as any government would do in a similar situation.

BEIJING'S POLICY

Beijing reiterates its policy regarding Taiwan's international role with each agreement it signs with other countries to establish diplomatic relations. The general principles in these agreements are the following:

(1) The country recognizes that there is only one China in the world, and Taiwan is part of China. (2) The country recognizes that the government of the People's Republic of China (PRC) is sole legal government of all China. Thus the country would not maintain or seek official relations with Taiwan. (3) The country maintains or seeks only economic and cultural relations with Taiwan. These principles or rules are clearly set in the communiqué for establishing diplomatic relations signed by the United States and China on December 16, 1978, and in the peace treaty between Japan and China that year. These principles are the same regarding international organizations to which Taiwan is or wants to be a member.

Under these principles, countries that have diplomatic relations with Beijing may also have economic and cultural ties with Taiwan. These economic and cultural ties can include signing agreements on trade, transportation, education, and cultural exchange; maintaining economic, cultural offices dealing with economic, cultural, and even consular matters; and Taiwan's participation in international economic and cultural organizations where statehood is not required. Under such principles and arrangements, Taiwan already has and enjoys significant international space. It has an economic and cultural office or a Taiwan representative office in almost every world capital. It participates in APEC (Asia-Pacific Economic Cooperation) and may enter the WTO (World Trade Organization). Its sports men and women attend the Olympics and other sports activities. Its business people engage in global trade and investment. Its people travel the world for tourism, study, and other activities.

Yet Taipei does not think it has enough international space. It wants something more. First, it wants not only economic and cultural but also political and security relations with foreign countries. It wants official relations with foreign governments. Its leaders want to travel abroad as governmental leaders and to pay official visits to foreign countries. Second, Taipei wants to participate not only in nonstatehood but also in state-membership-only international organizations such as the United Nations, World Bank, International Monetary Fund, and World Health Organization. Third, Taipei wants to take part in regional and international political-security activities such as KEDO (Korean Energy Development Organization) or the Asia-Pacific region missile defense system.

What Taipei wants is definitely unacceptable to Beijing. Taiwan's role and status in the international community are not those of a nation-state. The United Nations and the agreements signed between China and hundreds of countries and international organizations all recognize that Taiwan is not an independent state, that it is part of China. This is both principle and fact.

FUTURE TRENDS

Lee Teng-hui's "two-states" remark makes clear what he wants from Taiwan's international bid: independence. As Taiwan's intent clarifies, Beijing's position will likewise be clearer and tougher on Taiwan's international bid now and in the future.

First, Beijing will seek to deny Taiwan official international space with foreign countries. It will fight to limit the number of countries with which Taiwan has "diplomatic relations." There is now no basis for a "cease-fire." Time seems on the mainland's side. Mainland China will continue to grow, its economic and military power will increase, and its international status will rise. Therefore Beijing will have more leverage to woo others. With limited economic, political, diplomatic, and international resources, Taiwan's competitive capacity is limited. Taiwan is competing with an international giant, and this giant will be increasingly powerful and influential in the international community. Therefore, should the two sides across the strait no longer work for the dream of unification and determine to fight, the outcome is clear.

Second, Beijing will seek to deny Taiwan's space in official international organizations. There will be no room for Taiwan in the United Nations, World Health Organization, or any other international organization requiring statehood. The number of countries supporting Taiwan's bid to join the United Nations or other international organizations will decrease. When Taiwan forces others to choose between the mainland and Taiwan, few countries will choose Taipei.

Third, Beijing will seek to deny Taiwan additional space even in nongovernmental international organizations. The standard will be higher for Taiwan's entry; and when it enters, the space in those organizations will be more limited and restricted.

Finally, Beijing will seek to make life more difficult for those organizations of which Taiwan is already a member. Beijing will try to limit the space Taiwan already has. It will scrutinize anything regarding Taiwan in those organizational activities. It will definitely be more difficult for Taiwan to host future APEC meetings or even to host major international or regional sports activities such as the Asian Games.

SOLUTION?

Beijing does not wish to compete with Taipei over the issue of Taiwan's international space. Such competition costs both sides too much, and it gives others in the international community leverage over both sides. If zero-sum competition is not desirable for either side, what should be the solution? Two solutions seem desirable and workable.

Solution One: Maintain a One-China Framework

A one-China framework, although the two sides across the strait have never agreed on its exact meaning, has been a fundamental and limited consensus between the mainland and Taiwan. Beijing has proposed that "everything can be discussed under the principle of one China." Such actually refers to Beijing's position regarding Taiwan's international space. It means that if Taipei commits to remaining within a one-China framework, all other issues regarding Taiwan's international status and international space can be discussed and may find solution. Beijing has restated this position many times in past years, but Taipei has showed no interest. If Taipei agrees to "political talks" with Beijing and commits to maintaining a one-China principle, the next step would be to discuss Taiwan's international space, where the two sides could find agreement.

Solution Two: Maintain the Status Quo

The two sides across the Taiwan Strait have substantial differences on China (Lee Teng-hui does not want to talk about China), on one China, and on Taiwan's international status. If neither side across the strait can change the status quo, both should at least maintain it. Nobody is satisfied with the status quo. Taiwan wants to become more independent, if not totally independent. The mainland wants to increase ties with Taiwan and effect reunification. Both sides seem less patient with the status quo, but neither has the unilateral capability to change it. If either of the two tries seriously to challenge the status quo, such would not only fail but also create major difficulties for both sides.

Maintaining the status quo is not something either side prefers, but it is the best both can expect now or in the near future. If one cannot have what one wants, one should want what one has. This should be today's philosophy for both sides across the strait. If the status quo can be maintained, the relatively peaceful situation cross the strait can be maintained. In such a case, no major difficulties will arise and the two sides can work until a future solution can be determined.

Maintaining the status quo requires effort by both sides across the strait as well as cooperation from the international community, especially the United States, a country involved too long and too deeply in the cross-strait issue. Here another three no's may be necessary.

First, the Taiwan side should avoid creating another major crisis in cross-strait relations. In recent years, Lee Teng-hui, Taiwan's Democratic Progress Party, and other forces in Taiwan pursuing Taiwan's independence have created one crisis after other in cross-strait relations. In 1995, Lee Teng-hui damaged relations between the U.S. Congress and the U.S. administration by seeking to visit the United States. Lee's breakthrough caused a crisis between the mainland and Taiwan first, followed by a crisis between the United States and China. The two countries approached a military confrontation when the United States sent two aircraft carriers near the Taiwan area. Lee Teng-hui created another crisis in July 1999 when he defined the relationship between Taiwan and the mainland as "two-state relations" or "at least special state-to-state relations." To maintain the status quo, namely, peace and stability in the Taiwan Strait, Lee Teng-hui, the Democratic Progress Party, and others in Taiwan should stop creating crises across the strait. Otherwise, sooner or later, the status quo and peace and stability could be lost.

Second, the mainland may need to respond to Taiwan's independence moves more cautiously. The mainland needs various political, diplomatic, and even military actions to maintain the status quo of the Taiwan Strait. The mainland should watch carefully and be equally careful in reacting to cross-strait developments. Military action is one choice and the right of any country when protecting its national interest, including its national integration and national security. But the mainland should use its capabilities properly and in a timely fashion, avoiding overreaction.

Third, the international community, especially the United States, needs to be more restrained so as not to support or encourage those making trouble across the strait. This includes caution regarding military arms, missile defense, or rhetorical protection of Taiwan from within the U.S. Congress or government. Otherwise, words or actions by officials in the United States, Japan, or elsewhere could encourage some in Taiwan to go further in breaking the status quo and thus create a crisis for both sides across the strait and for the international community.

CONCLUSION

The only possible and desirable solution to the Taiwan issue must come from the two sides. The Taiwan issue should be decided and resolved by the Chinese people living on both sides of the strait. The solution will derive from economic, political, and social developments on both sides. As both sides continue to change and develop, one can only hope that those changes and developments will bring the two sides closer, allowing them to resolve their differences more easily than they can do today. Change and development need time. Therefore, before the two sides can draw close enough to overcome fundamental differences, the best policy is for each to maintain the status quo and thereby maintain peace and security across the Taiwan Strait.

CHAPTER FIVE

THE TWO-STATE THEORY: MYTH OR REALITY?

Zhao Gancheng

THE TAIWAN QUESTION IS HEATING UP AGAIN across the Taiwan Strait and in northeast Asia after Lee Teng-hui stated his two-state theory, which cast dark shadows on prospects for regional peace and stability.[1] Given developments, the current institutional structure for peaceful coexistence and ultimately for cross-strait unification seems in danger of collapse. It is not meaningful to ask who is to blame for this situation. But the apparent trigger has been the unexpected challenge by Taiwan's leaders to the political basis of bilateral exchanges and the existing regime, namely, the mainland's Association for Relations Across the Taiwan Strait and Taiwan's Straits Exchange Foundation. In fact, Wang Daohan's proposed first visit to Taiwan has been canceled, and the cross-strait relationship is again stalemated.

There are many arguments from Taiwan's officials and experts alike in defending the theory. No doubt, the theory needs to be defended, but defending points must be reasonable and rational. Herein lies a basic question: Do the two sides want or are they willing to seek peaceful coexistence before making any substantial moves? Taipei rebukes Beijing's calls for one country, two systems. Beijing never says whether, if Taipei does not accept it, Beijing will use force to intimidate Taipei into submission. In other words, Beijing can accept the status quo as long as both sides maintain a one-China principle. Beijing does not like the status quo, but it does not make unilateral moves to pressure the other side. It is Taiwan that tries to break the status quo and, unfortunately, on the basis of denying the one-China principle, a common stance that has been accepted by both sides for a long time. Common sense suggests that Taiwan's attempts at a breakthrough must have rational reasons. Let us consider five.

TAIWAN'S SOVEREIGNTY AND LEGITIMATE REPRESENTATIVE

Taiwan argues that its relations with the People's Republic of China (PRC) constitute state-to-state relations because the PRC has never ruled Taiwan. It is true that the PRC has never ruled the island since its founding, but direct governance is not a necessary condition in defining the sovereignty of a certain territory and, in this case, the sovereignty of the legitimate Chinese government on Taiwan. The Republic of China (ROC), founded in 1912, never ruled Taiwan before it resumed sovereignty of the island from Japanese colonial rule in 1946. This did not prevent the international community from guaranteeing the island's sovereignty to China through international treaties and declarations. Note that Taiwan's sovereignty was guaranteed to China; the ROC took it only because then it was the only legitimate representative of China. Otherwise the communist government, in Yan'an of northwest China at that time, could have had the right to it too. Therefore the sovereignty of Taiwan belongs to China and must be taken by the legitimate representative of China according to relevant international treaties.

If Taiwan yet insists that the ROC has sovereignty on Taiwan, such a ruling would be insufficient, just as Japan's ruling the island did not constitute Tokyo's sovereignty. Taiwan has to prove it is the sole legitimate representative of China. This legal difficulty requires the Taiwan regime to look for alternatives, as it has done for decades. In a legal sense, Taiwan's authorities cannot escape this dilemma. It explains why Lee's predecessors stuck to one China when the PRC did not rule the island either. Now Lee wants to change that. Would he also be able to change relevant articles of international treaties? The answer is no. Would he be able to resume the ROC's status as the only legitimate representative of China as it was from 1912 to 1949? The answer is again no. Thus what Lee wants is a serious challenge to both the international community and China's territorial integrity.

It is widely believed that his ultimate motive is to make the island independent. Such a unilateral move, without warning but involving China's fundamental interests, provokes unnecessary tension in northeast Asia and eventually jeopardizes the interests of all relevant regional parties. At a "summit" with Central American and Caribbean states in Taipei on September 7, 1999, Lee argued that "truth and justice would prevail eventually."[2] But the truth is apparent, and justice has been carried out from the viewpoint of the international community, that is, the return of sovereignty over Taiwan to China after Japan's colonial rule. The type of justice Lee wants to pursue cannot but violate international law and thus jeopardize the fundamental interests of all Chinese people.

DO EQUAL TALKS REQUIRE STATEHOOD?

Taiwan argues that it must have equal status with the mainland in talks on political affairs. Therefore the two-state theory is an assertion of that sort of equality. But, if Taiwan's authorities still adhere to the one-China principle as many Taiwan scholars agree they do, do equal talks among different parties within one nation require the statehood of the location of these parties? Beijing has persistently called for equal talks among all relevant parties in China, whether or not a ruling party, precisely because China's reunification is the concern of all Chinese people. The reason is quite clear. Such talks would include important matters: the definition of China, the status of Taiwan in the international community and its international space before unification, and the reduction of mutual distrust and an emphasis on confidence-building measures between the different political systems across the strait. These matters must be equal among all the relevant parties. This is not new. As early as 1984, Deng Xiaoping in an interview stressed the importance of equal talks between the two ruling parties, the Chinese Communist Party and the Kuomintang. (The Democratic Progressive Party [DPP] had not yet been founded.) Deng also pointed out that, in any cross-strait talks, words such as "central" or "local" should not be used to refer to either party.[3]

Taiwan does not trust Beijing's initiatives. Given this lack of confidence, Beijing can do little to move ahead. Common sense tells us that any serious negotiations must require a minimum of confidence. While rejecting Beijing's call for equal talks on political matters, Taiwan has unilaterally challenged the process by asserting state-to-state relations.

The dilemma of the two-state theory for equality is that, as a sovereign state, Taiwan would have equal standing not only with the PRC but also with all the states in the world. But as a state, Taiwan, like Singapore where the Chinese are the majority of the population, would not need to have political talks with the PRC. Who would say that Singapore needs to have political talks with the PRC for the definition of China, or the status of Singapore in the international community, or whatever? Therefore, with regard to political talks across the strait, the two-state theory destroys any necessity for such talks and any possibility for them as well. This is exactly what Beijing argues is the danger of Taiwan's permanent split from China, if Beijing accepts the two-state theory. The issue is not whether relevant parties are equal in possible talks. They are certainly equal by any criterion. The issue is whether Taiwan remains part of China. Part of China is not necessarily part of the PRC, because the PRC has never argued that Taiwan is part of the PRC or that it must be ruled by the PRC.

The internationally recognized three principles regarding Taiwan are the following: "There is but one China in the world"; "Taiwan is part of China"; and "The PRC is the sole legitimate government of China." The third principle strongly depicts the PRC as the legal representative of China in the international community, but it does not necessarily mean that Taiwan must be ruled by the PRC. This is the logical starting point of the "one country, two systems" formula.

Taiwan scholars argue that Taiwan as part of China would logically lead only to Taiwan being part of the PRC. But this is strange logic. According to many statements by PRC leaders, China's ultimate form of unification is far from being determined. Even the one-country, two-systems formula is only an initiative, and many issues remain to be discussed. When even a first step, such as political talks across the strait, encounters difficulties, Taiwan's real motives remain questionable. The two-state theory is driven not by the desire for an equal negotiating status but to betray the one-China principle while seeking Taiwan's independence.

SOLUTION TO INTERNATIONAL SPACE

International space has been a contentious issue across the strait, increasing distrust between the two sides. The biggest challenge to international space lies in whether the Chinese themselves across the strait can solve relevant disputes. It is not whether Taiwan's 22 million people should enjoy dignity in the international community. By keeping and expanding economic and cultural exchanges, Taiwan will never lose dignity. But if the two sides across the strait fail to solve their disputes, the international-space issue will persist and the outcome will be more serious than simply Taiwan's identity.

Since Taiwan's unilateral declaration of itself as a state cannot be a solution, other scenarios may be relevant.

The first is armed conflict. This could arise if Beijing rejects Taiwan's declaration and uses all means including force to stop it. Leaving aside who would win, as far as the international community is concerned, any recognition of an independent Taiwan before settlement by the Chinese themselves would be risky, hence unlikely. Then the dispute would return to its starting point. Unless the Chinese themselves across the strait reach mutual understanding and compromise, the international community would find it difficult to do anything substantial. In other words, even after paying an almost unbearable cost, the issue of the international space of Taiwan would remain as questionable as before.

The second is competition short of conflict. It is possible for the PRC not to accept Taiwan's declaration, or to use force, but to use all other means to oppose Taiwan's international initiatives. Again this would hypothetically produce either of two situations. Facing great countermeasures from the PRC, the international community would cautiously wait and hope that the Chinese themselves could reach solid agreement on the basis of mutual understanding and compromise. Until then the international community would not accept Taiwan as an independent state. This is the situation now. Alternatively, the international community, regardless of the PRC's countermeasures, could accept Taiwan as an independent sovereign state. Because the PRC would adhere to its stance, Beijing would have no choice but to cut off diplomatic relations with countries that accept Taiwan as an independent sovereign state. Such would hurt the PRC, but not benefit anyone, except perhaps Taiwan's "international space."

By its nature, before settlement of the Taiwan issue by the Chinese themselves across the strait, the issue of Taiwan's international space is basically a zero-sum game. The two-state theory will not change that. Taiwan's experience in this regard in recent years has been bitter. Some of Taiwan's scholars, such as Chien-min Chao of National Chengchi University, Taipei, argue that "Taiwan has been deprived of the right of carrying on the name of China," so why should it be part of China? This argument is unfair and inaccurate. For example, in the Olympic Games, Taiwan's team bears the name Chinese Taipei, which constitutes name sharing, but is unsatisfactory only to Taiwan. Moreover this situation is attributable to Taiwan's persistence in not negotiating with the PRC. The PRC has sought political talks with Taiwan. According to Jiang Zemin's eight points, under a one-China principle, the two sides can discuss anything. This would seem to include the status of Taiwan in the international community before unification. Unfortunately, Taiwan refuses political talks while seeking more international space, indeed while seeking membership in a number of international organizations that require statehood, including the United Nations.

There is no doubt that Taiwan's consistent refusal of political talks with the PRC and its endless efforts put the PRC in a difficult situation. Compromise and concession are required if the people in Taiwan are to have a legitimate position in the international community before any cross-strait final settlement, without violation of the one-China principle. Such requires mutual effort. For example, after mutual concessions, Taiwan's finance minister attended the 1989 annual meeting of the Asian Development Bank in Beijing with finance ministers of member states of the organization. Taiwan's circumscribed participation in APEC (the Asia-Pacific Economic Cooperation) is another example.

This is not to argue that such arrangements are good for Taiwan or fully reflect Taiwan's representation in international organizations. This issue needs serious cross-strait discussion. But unilateral actions that hurt the interests of the other party do not work, including the two-state theory. Further stalemate will only increase cross-strait distrust and tension. It is inconceivable that tenser cross-strait relations will give Taiwan more international space.

DEMOCRACY: IRRELEVANT TO SOVEREIGNTY

Defenders of Taiwan's separation from China probably use democracy most frequently as the reason for their defense. No doubt similar political systems across the strait would facilitate a unified nation. But again political unity is not a necessary condition for China's sovereignty. The different political systems across the strait are the product of China's historical development, the civil war in the 1940s, and the subsequent Cold War international environment. The former split China and the latter helped consolidate different political systems across the strait. According to international law, a nation's social system is irrelevant to the nation's sovereignty. In China's case, the different political systems across the strait can be regarded only as its internal affair. How to solve these differences can rest only on the political wisdom and will of the people of that nation-state. In this sense, Lee's two-state theory based on a difference in political systems across the strait must be seen as a serious abuse of the nation-state's sovereignty.

The PRC has never opposed the political system chosen by Taiwan's people. They have a right to choose any political system that they believe will be good for them. By the same token, the mainland's political system is also the outcome of an historic process. There are reasons for the ideological disputes between the mainland and Taiwan, which have sometimes been fierce over the past half-century. The collapse of the former Soviet Union did not reduce these disputes as some expected. On the contrary, the PRC has come under more out-side pressure. In this context, by shifting to a universal voting system, Taiwan tried to use democracy to reach its political goal. Using democracy to advocate a separate Taiwan may have a limited future for several reasons:

- The dispute across the strait stems from and focuses on sovereignty, which, according to international law, is indivisible. The dispute is not about ideology or political systems. Hence, using the differences in political systems to deny the one-China principle misses the core issues and is invalid.

- Different political systems reflect only different developmental stages. They do not automatically or naturally determine which is superior and which is inferior. Given cross-strait realities, "one country, two systems" has its own rationale. Simply denying that rationale does not necessarily show Taiwan's self-superiority.

- Both socialism and liberalism are ideologies imported from the West to China. Viewed historically, imported ideology will not be valid in China until it adapts itself to Chinese culture and tradition. In this context, the PRC calls on all relevant parties to give up ideological bias and to discuss political issues across the strait on a purely equal basis. China is larger and more deeply rooted than these ideological disputes. But the two-state theory argues for an independent state of Taiwan based on ideology.

Arguing the difference in political systems across the strait should also be seen as Taipei's attempt to unify China on Taiwan's terms. This constitutes a precondition set by Taiwan. Taiwan's authorities often accuse the PRC of setting preconditions for cross-strait talks. It is true that preconditions usually play a negative role in negotiations. But, compared with a one-China principle, Taiwan's claim that China can be unified only in a political system similar to that of Taiwan constitutes a large and more serious precondition for talks across the strait. This precondition is an obstacle.

Ideological dispute still plays a significant role in bilateral relations. Many arguments in both Taiwan and Western countries show an ideological bias. The two-state theory derives from a dispute that has lasted more than a half-century. No one expects to eliminate it overnight. But as the world changes, new approaches may be given a chance to escape the traps of mutual accusation and the dilemmas of stalemate.

PUBLIC OPINION: A DOUBLE-EDGED SWORD

Public opinion is another controversial element in cross-strait relations. It is not only emotional but also often misleading in terms of possible consequences. For example, after the statement of the two-state theory, the Association of Euro-Asian Studies in Taiwan conducted a poll in late July. The outcome showed that 73 percent of the people in Taiwan support the status of two states regarding relations across the strait. Such poll results are frequently quoted by both the ruling and the opposition parties as well as by Taiwan's media.

At the same time, a poll in Beijing in early August 1999 by the *China Youth Daily*, a leading mainland newspaper, found that 82 percent of respondents supported the PRC government's use of force against Taiwan if Taipei became independent. The newspaper argued, from poll results, that ignoring the increasing trend of Taiwan independence would be a serious mistake. The permanent split of Taiwan from China would be a loss that China could never afford and the Chinese people would never tolerate.

As argued by Pei-hwa Pai of the DPP mission in the United Sates in her commentary in the *Taiwan International Review*, public opinion should be respected and followed by political leadership.[4] That journal in the same volume went further to say that 89 percent of the people in Taiwan disagree that the island should be part of China.

Without doubt, political leaders must consider public opinion while remaining cautious about polls. Given Taiwan Strait sensitivities and risks, an improper announcement of poll results could be misleading. For example, the disparate results from polls in Taipei and Beijing do not safely tell political leaders what steps to take next. If the leadership on either side closely follows such polls, armed conflict could arise. All this argues that public opinion can be a volatile double-edged sword.

Public opinion can be misleading. In the case of the Taiwan question, because it has lasted more than a half-century, mutual distrust between the two sides is deep. Propaganda by the two sides can only worsen the situation. Overuse of public opinion may undermine stability and the ability to promote a peaceful solution.

At this moment, which is critical in cross-strait relations, wisdom and common sense by leaders across the strait are needed. Common sense says that no one wants armed conflict. It also says that the Taiwan question is particularly complex, involving the fundamental interests of relevant parties. Therefore unilateral moves to force the other party to answer yes or no will not work, whether or not supported by public opinion. Political wisdom requires proper approaches to complex issues that consider the interests of all relevant parties. In this sense, Lee's unilateral move to impose his two-state theory on other relevant parties deliberately ignores their interests. This is not limited to the PRC's interests but includes U.S. interest in Asia-Pacific regional stability.

COMMON GOAL: AVOIDING ARMED CONFLICT

The above analysis seeks to clarify the myth of the two-state theory. This myth will not end soon, even though it does not have the power to become reality. Lee Teng-hui will not retract his theory; the PRC will not accept the two-state theory as the basis of cross-strait political talks. The short-term outlook is likely to be a stalemate. As a first step all relevant parties desperately need to avoid armed conflict across the strait.

People on Taiwan always argue that the PRC threatens Taiwan's security because the PRC will not renounce the use of force. But they seldom point out that the PRC upholds peaceful unification unless Taiwan becomes independent.[5] This policy is based on the concept that everyone across the strait is Chinese. We do not need another civil war to resolve Taiwan's status. But, as argued by Lee, Taiwan should be an independent and sovereign state, which could mean only that it no longer thinks of itself as Chinese. In that case, from the PRC's perspective, China's fundamental national interests are jeopardized. Does Taiwan have the power and the right to force the PRC to accept its proposition on a unilateral basis?

Furthermore the Taiwan question is a complex issue left over from history. The long-lasting split of the island from China is the result of the political wills not only of the two sides across the strait but also of various international elements including U.S. involvement. Therefore the interactions across the strait should also cause great concern for the United States. This is why the United States has proposed interim agreements and the Taiwan Security Enhancement Act is being discussed on Capitol Hill. In fact, what the United States does with regard to Taiwan is closely and sometimes nervously watched by both sides across the strait.

But merely elaborating the respective positions of relevant parties may neither prevent an armed conflict across the strait nor necessarily build confidence. The key to avoiding armed conflict may lie in preventive measures determined by the relevant parties, in this case, Taiwan, the PRC, and the United States.

Since Taiwan's authorities precipitated the crisis of the two-state theory, some wonder about Taipei's sincerity in maintaining peace and stability in the strait. Lee might move even further ahead, depending on his perception of the responses of the PRC and the United States. Lee's interpretation that the PRC is "too unstable, with too many problems, to attack Taiwan" only adds to the tension.[6] The judgment of many is that Lee will not move further.[7] If that is the case, the two-state theory will not change the status quo, only produce a stalemate. A stalemate, although a serious setback to cross-strait relations, is preferable to armed conflict. The international community therefore has a stake in Lee's taking no further steps regarding the two-state theory. Faced with a stalemate resulting from Taiwan's pursuit of independent and sovereign status, the PRC does not have much room. The flexibility of the PRC's Taiwan policy has been reduced to a dangerous point.

But its bottom line is keeping the island part of China. If Taiwan were no longer sovereign, there would be nothing left for the PRC to talk about with the Taiwan regime, and no leadership of the PRC could possibly afford to let the island go. It is in this context that the

PRC does not and will not renounce use of force precisely because on the island the trend toward independence is dramatically increasing. Renouncing the use of force as the last resort would be equivalent to giving up its efforts for unification. This point must be made clear, and whether the bottom line is acknowledged or accepted by Taiwan is irrelevant.

With regard to the policy of the United States, a number of Taiwan's scholars and officials argue that the two-state theory was partially the result of the Clinton administration's China policy, particularly the three no's that President Clinton stated in Shanghai during his first visit to the PRC in 1998. There are no real grounds for this conclusion, and it should be regarded as an excuse. The United States has not changed its China policy with regard to the Taiwan question. The essence of the U.S. position on Taiwan remains unchanged, despite shifts and statements reflecting changes in the international environment. The essence is never to let Taiwan fall into the hands of an enemy. From that basic position, U.S. policy toward Taiwan is both flexible and ambiguous, serving a strategic goal of neither war nor unification. It may be an exaggeration to say that U.S. policy seeks to manipulate the two sides across the strait, but the status quo certainly favors U.S. interests. Lee's challenge to the status quo could create difficulties for the United States.

The current cross-strait stalemate also reduces the role of the United States. The paradox for the United States is that Washington can control neither the PRC nor Taiwan, but actions and moves by either side can pull the United States into complicated situations. Therefore, keeping its commitments is its most reliable option. This is also why President Clinton reiterated a one-China policy soon after Lee's latest challenge. Some U.S. scholars argue that Clinton's statement "tilted U.S. policy farther in China's favor."[8] But no U.S. administration would adopt policies in China's favor unless they were in the interest of the United States. Thus avoiding both unification and armed conflict will remain in U.S. interests. That is precisely the goal of the proposed interim agreement, so far rejected by both sides across the strait. But the United States has the leverage to maintain the status quo. The question is whether it has the political will to use it properly. That the United States no longer has a bipartisan China policy makes it harder for the administration to play a role in the cross-strait dispute.

In the current environment, challenges to the status quo have come from Taiwan. Although the United States does not control Taiwan, Washington has great influence on Taiwan's decisionmaking. Facing the rhetoric of Lee and other Taiwan leaders and the fierce response of the PRC, President Clinton and other senior U.S. officials reiterated the one-China policy of the United States.[9] But the United States may have to do still more to prevent the situation from deteriorating further. Continuing sales of advanced weapons to Taiwan only encourages the independence trend on the island. Actually, a cross-strait war would reduce U.S. leverage. Confronting Washington with a "yes" or "no" question would not benefit U.S. interests.

LASTING PEACE AND STABILITY

In addition to crisis-management policies, which are critical now, the Taiwan question requires serious consideration of a more sophisticated arrangement to secure lasting peace and stability in the strait, whether governmental or nongovernmental. The existing quasi-governmental mechanism works, sometimes quite effectively. Preventing military conflict, maintaining control, and reducing miscalculations should also be on the agenda. The current stalemate makes it hard to work within the existing mechanism, let alone to build new mechanisms, although confidence-building mechanisms are important.

Both sides need to communicate at a certain military level to reduce out-of-control encounters and miscalculation. The reason is simple. The PRC does not renounce use of force, but it does not necessarily want war. The official claim of the Taiwan authorities is that their ultimate goal is also a unified China. From this common point both sides should also have the political will to maintain at least the status quo while seeking limited goals such as some type of CBMS (continental ballistic missile system) at the military level.

Another significant variable is Taiwan's election in March 2000. It is generally acknowledged that Lee Teng-hui has played a personal and decisive role in Taiwan's policy regarding cross-strait relations. Therefore his successor will certainly have an influence, for better or worse. But even if Chen Shui-bian, the DPP candidate, is elected, all constraints regarding the Taiwan question would remain. In this sense, the basics of the issue would remain, requiring a process as complex as it has been, no matter who is elected.

In conclusion, the Taiwan question cannot be solved through unilateral moves such as Lee's unexpected two-state theory. In most cases, unilateral moves increase difficulties and tensions in cross-strait relations. The two-state theory and the subsequent stalemate again illustrate this point, as Lee's "private visit" to the United Sates did in 1995. Although the myth the theory has created is destructive, it will not last long, it is hoped. To maintain Asia-Pacific peace and stability and for the sake of the fundamental interests of all the Chinese across the strait, political leaders must show courage and wisdom. They can do so by stopping further provocations of the other party; by continuing and even expanding nongovernmental and business exchanges including the three links to re-create an earlier atmosphere; by keeping the working framework alive, given the postponement of Wang Daohan's visit to Taiwan; and by exploring ways to develop confidence-building mechanisms, particularly in the military field, when conditions are right.

Notes

1. The Taiwan authorities, after his statement, interpreted Lee's theory as "special state-to-state relations," which might produce some slight difference from what Lee stated previously, but the nature of the statement and its purpose remain unchanged. I use the term "two-state theory" as the mainland's media have done, not only for this reason but also to facilitate the discussion.

2. *South China Morning Post,* September 7, 1999.

3. Su Ge, *U. S. China Policy and Taiwan Question,* Chinese ed. (1999), 554. The original text of Deng's view is seen in the *Selected Works of Deng Xiaoping,* vol. 3, Chinese ed., Beijing, 30–31.

4. *Taiwan International Review* 5, issue 3 (May–June 1999).

5. There are also other conditions set by the PRC, including severe interference of foreign forces in Taiwan and significant chaos on the island. But this article for analytical purposes will focus on the problem of independence, given the current development in cross-strait relationships.

6. *South China Morning Post,* September 10, 1999. Lee made that estimate at a gathering of ruling Kuomintang cadres in southern Tainan county on September 9 after a two-month war of words with the PRC.

7. But this is quite uncertain. According to the latest development in September, Lee seems to be pushing hard behind the scenes for abolishing the current "constitution" and formulating a "basic law" or something like it. If true, this would appear to seek legalizing his two-state theory by writing it into a new framework. This is dangerous because it would be seen as equivalent to declaring independence.

8. Stephen J. Yates, *Punishing the Victim: The Clinton Administration's Rebuke of Taiwan,* Heritage Foundation executive memorandum 617, August 3, 1999.

9. On September 16, the U.S. representative to the UN, for the first time in seven years, said at a UN committee that the United States adheres to a one-China policy and would not support Taiwan's participation in the organization, a clear signal that the two-state theory is not to be accepted by the international community.

CHAPTER SIX

TAIWAN'S LEGAL STATUS: BEYOND THE UNIFICATION– INDEPENDENCE DICHOTOMY

Philip Yang

TAIWAN'S AMBIGUOUS STATUS IN INTERNATIONAL LAW is a product of a half-century of changing international and cross-strait circumstances. Geopolitics and the PRC's claim to sovereignty over Taiwan also affect the status of Taiwan and bilateral relations across the Taiwan Strait. According to international legal theories and practices, the long nonrecognition by most countries in the world also contributes to Taiwan's dilemma. Nonrecognition is due partly to the political nature of the international law of recognition and partly to misunderstanding the traditional idea of sovereignty in international law.

Here I discuss traditional conditions for statehood with respect to Taiwan. I also propose a new approach and a framework to democratic sovereignty. This new approach to democratic sovereignty, both internal and external, is then applied to the case of Taiwan to determine Taiwan's international legal status and its legal personality and capacity. Finally I discuss the meaning of "one China" and relations between the two political entities across the Taiwan Strait, arguing that, although bilateral political and private law relations remain unique and special circumstances apply, China and Taiwan are two separate states in political and legal reality.

TAIWAN AND TRADITIONAL CONDITIONS FOR STATEHOOD: ANOTHER TAIWAN EXPERIENCE

The government of the Republic of China (ROC) on Taiwan remains in effective control of an area of 14,000 square miles and more than 22 million people, each earning an average of U.S.$11,500 a year. Taiwan is the world's 14th-largest trading nation and holds the world's third-largest foreign-exchange reserve. The "Taiwan experience" was originally used to refer to Taiwan's rapid economic development. Since the late 1980s, the movement toward political liberalization and democratization in Taiwan has attracted more attention than its economic miracle. The meaning of the Taiwan experience has thus expanded to include Taiwan's stable political democratization.

Taiwan is not recognized diplomatically by most countries of the world; it has not been represented in the United Nations or other major international intergovernmental organizations since China's seat in the UN was awarded to the Beijing government in 1971. Yet, owing to its economic strength and political achievements, Taiwan has maintained substantive or functional relations with most countries in the world and has participated, under different names, in some important international economic organizations. Taiwan's ambiguous international status, diplomatic isolation, and close substantive relations with other states constitute "another Taiwan experience."

A state as a juristic person in international law should possess four qualifications: a permanent population, a defined territory, a government, and the capacity to enter into relations with other states.[1] Satisfaction of the first three qualifications is a matter of fact, not law. As far as public international law is concerned, the last qualification, the capacity to engage in formal relations with other states, is most important and controversial.

Before the 1971 UN resolution that accorded China's UN seat to the PRC in Beijing, Taiwan was recognized by almost half of the world's countries. Now Taiwan has diplomatic relations with 28 states. Yet Taiwan also maintains substantive relations, including semiofficial, commercial, trade, and cultural relations, with more than 140 states in the world.² Taiwan sends diplomats and trade representatives all over the globe to promote such unofficial relations with other countries. The ROC on Taiwan therefore has an unquestioned capacity to engage in foreign relations with other nations. Even scholars who do not regard Taiwan as a sovereign state acknowledge that "Taiwan was under the de facto authority of a government that engaged in foreign relations and entered into international agreements with other governments."³

Facts and legal analysis indicate that Taiwan fulfills all the traditional criteria for statehood. It has a clearly defined territorial base, an island larger in size than 90 states in the world; 22 million people permanently living within its territory; a stable, effective, and popularly elected government; and the capacity and willingness to engage in relations with other states. According to these international legal criteria, the word "state" has a clear meaning and appears entirely applicable to Taiwan.

DEMOCRATIC SOVEREIGNTY: NEW APPROACH

Sovereignty is central to the study of both the nature of the modern state and the theory of international law. It has therefore a dual connotation: within the state and in international law or, respectively, internal and external. The idea of sovereignty began as an indication of the political power enjoyed by a prince within a state. Later it came to describe both internal and external power relations. The external application of sovereignty became a core concept of international law and relations more quickly than it did in the domestic context. Sovereignty cannot be fully understood without reference to its specific context in time and space. Changes in the doctrine of sovereignty reflect changes in political facts, both domestic and international.

Sovereignty remains a constitutive concept although its principles are neither fixed nor constant.⁴ In the domestic application, internal sovereignty denotes constitutional arrangements regulating the balance of power state authority upholds. In the international context, external sovereignty means a state's independence from other states and the exclusive jurisdiction over its subjects within its territory. ⁵

FRAMEWORK FOR DEMOCRATIC SOVEREIGNTY

A new concept of democratic sovereignty and a preliminary framework for this new approach as the legal basis of state jurisdiction integrate the domestic and the international applications of the notion of sovereignty.

Although sovereignty in the domestic or constitutional context is closely related to sovereignty in international law, few scholars connect the two concepts. Herein lies the major difference between the new approach to sovereignty and previous approaches. The new approach seeks to synthesize discussions about sovereignty both in political theory and in international law. Unlike other approaches that discuss either the development from absolute to popular sovereignty or the relationship between autonomy and independence, the new approach integrates the dual connotation of sovereignty—within the state and in international law.

Internal Sovereignty

Internal sovereignty, which refers to sovereignty's domestic sense, and internal autonomy, which is the internal aspect of sovereignty in international law, have close theoretical connections. That is, based on possession of the final political and legal power, a sovereign state holds the highest legal authority within its territorial domain. The internal dimension of the idea of democratic sovereignty includes democratic governance, a constitutional legal system, and domestic jurisdiction.

Democratic governance. Democratic sovereignty means not only that sovereignty should reside with the people but also that the legitimacy of democratic governance is recognized. Democratic sovereignty denotes both the substantive and the procedural legitimacy of democratic governance in the internal political structure of a state. The concepts of both absolute and popular sovereignty are defined by the location and distribution of decisionmaking and lawmaking power. Because popular sovereignty merely transfers the absolute rule of the monarch to the absolute rule of the people, it could lead to anarchy or to despotism of the few in the name of the many. Indeed, the past 200 years have seen many cases of politicians using the people's name while exercising dictatorial rule.

Constitutional legal system. The internal aspect of sovereignty in international law means that a state has the highest legal authority within its territorial boundary. This legal authority is not subject to the governmental, executive, legislative, or judicial jurisdiction of a foreign state or any foreign law other than international law. This aspect of sovereignty is also known as territorial sovereignty, which means the complete and exclusive authority a state exercises over all persons and things found on, under, or above its territory. An autonomous state therefore will have its own legal system that can exercise exclusive jurisdiction over individuals and property within its territory. The requirement of a legal system is the basis for a sovereign state to be independent from another nation's legal control. In other words, the constitutional legal system, which is not subject to another state's control, constitutes a state's internal autonomy.

Domestic jurisdiction. Sovereignty also denotes the basic international legal quality of a state and an attribute of statehood. Therefore sovereignty should be viewed as the legal basis for the competence and restriction of state jurisdiction. As Rebecca Wallance points out, "jurisdiction is an attribute of state sovereignty."[6] Jurisdiction is primarily exercised on a territorial basis for "the territory of a state furnishes the title for the competence of the state."[7] Territorial limits on state competence are not absolute; a state may occasionally exercise jurisdiction outside its territory.

External Sovereignty

External sovereignty traditionally refers to its international application. In the past, scholars have not given sufficient weight to the development of the idea of sovereignty in the domestic sense. Instead they tend to apply only the absolute aspect of state authority to the theory of sovereignty in international law. For the new approach to democratic sovereignty described here, external sovereignty is the external application of the idea of sovereignty as a whole. It includes external independence, extraterritorial jurisdiction, and sovereign rights and immunities.

External independence. The external aspect of democratic sovereignty in international law underlines the independence and equality of states and the fact that they are direct and immediate subjects of international law. According to James Crawford, "it seems preferable to restrict 'independence' to the prerequisite for statehood, and 'sovereignty' to the legal incident."[8] In other words, independence, like the existence of population, a territory, and a government, is a precondition for the existence of a state, whereas sovereignty is the attribute of statehood once it has been established.

Sovereign rights and immunities. Based on external sovereignty, a state can enjoy, in accordance with international law, certain rights and immunities outside its territorial domain. Sovereign rights, a relatively new concept developed from the law of the sea, refer to the rights of coastal states with regard to exploring, exploiting, conserving, and managing the natural resources of the continental shelf and the Exclusive Economic Zone. The word "sovereign" is used to characterize rights that are exclusive in the sense that if the coastal state does not explore or exploit its resources, no other state can undertake activities to do so without the coastal state's express consent. The rights do not depend on occupation, effective or notional, or on any express proclamation.

Extraterritorial jurisdiction. External sovereignty is the legal basis for a state's extraterritorial jurisdiction, which may be based on the effects principle, passive personality principle, protective principle, or universality principle. Based on the legal competence of external sovereignty, states also enjoy sovereign immunity for their public actions. Moreover certain sovereign rights belong exclusively to states.

TAIWAN: DEMOCRATIC SOVEREIGNTY

Here I consider Taiwan's legal status within the new approach to democratic sovereignty outlined above. The theory provides a framework for examining all the other formal features of an entity and for deciding whether it constitutes a democratic form of government. Internal sovereignty includes political democratization, a constitutional legal system, a policymaking process, and domestic jurisdiction. External sovereignty includes external independence, diplomatic efforts, and extraterritorial jurisdiction. From them one can determine whether the ROC on Taiwan is a sovereign state by using a more objective and sophisticated method than traditionally used to approach this issue.

Internal Sovereignty of Taiwan

As discussed above, the internal aspect of democratic sovereignty entails three features: democratic governance, the constitutional legal system, and domestic jurisdiction. Examining Taiwan's constitutional development, recent political democratization, policymaking process, and the legal system on which its domestic jurisdiction is based argues for a mature democratic sovereignty in Taiwan's internal political structure. Also, examining Taiwan's constitutional development and its legal system argues that the people and government of the ROC on Taiwan hold the final political and legal power, in other words, the highest political and legal authority within Taiwan's territorial domain.

Political democratization. Taiwan's political democratization took place in a unique social–historical context. Taiwan's successful economic development fostered the emergence and development of a pluralistic society sufficiently strong to exert pressures on the political system to be more responsible. There was a reduction in Taiwan Strait tension in the late 1970s, and there were social and economic developments within Taiwan and abroad.[9] Therefore the Kuomintang leadership realized that liberalization and democratization had become not only the fervent desire of many people but also an urgent necessity if the country was to meet future development goals.[10] Taiwan today has meaningful and extensive competition for government power through all levels of regular elections. Opposition parties of real significance exist. Considerable civil and political liberties, including freedoms of expression, of the press, to form organizations, and to demonstrate and strike, are common features of public and political life.[11]

Policymaking process. After four decades of industrialization and economic growth, Taiwan's social structure has become highly differentiated. Taiwan's policymaking process is open. As in any other democratic country, many channels exist for citizen involvement in policymaking, at least for nonstrategic policies. In most cases, three organizations at different levels formulate policy—the bureaucracy, the Executive Yuan Council, and the Central Standing Committee of the ruling party, the Kuomintang.[12] Thus the preference of the people, the lobbying of interest groups, and the opinions of intellectuals all play important roles.

Constitutional legal system and domestic jurisdiction. Domestic jurisdiction refers to the competence of the state to govern persons and property by its municipal law, both criminal and civil, within its territorial domain and subject to the limits of international law. The competence of state jurisdiction depends on an independent and comprehensive legal system. Taiwan's legal system is close to the civil law system and based largely on German, Swiss, and Japanese models and experiences. Therefore much of the law is codified to provide a framework for legal transactions and relationships. Bills are submitted by the Executive Yuan to the Legislative Yuan; the legislation contains provisions that delegate authority to the various ministries, councils, and commissions of the Executive Yuan to implement statutory provisions through detailed regulations and guidelines.

External Sovereignty of Taiwan

External sovereignty traditionally refers to the international manifestation of the idea of sovereignty. In Taiwan's case, one can examine Taiwan's external independence and its sovereign rights and immunities.

External independence. Independence may be seen as sovereignty's external aspect. The concept entails the state's legal right generally to conduct its own affairs without direction, interference, or control by any other state. The ROC on Taiwan is self-governing under its own constitution and legal system, which are not under the control of any other state's constitutional arrangement. The ROC has a territory base and support of the population and is recognized by a stable number of countries.

One indicator of an entity's possession of an independent international personality is its independent treaty-making capacity. The ROC on Taiwan has independently entered all kinds of political, military, economic, commercial, cultural, and technical agreements with foreign states. Most agreements involve the exercise of government power. The ROC on Taiwan has also maintained its status as a party to some multilateral treaties.

Sovereign rights and immunities. States can enjoy, based on external sovereignty, in accordance with international law, certain rights and immunities outside their territorial domains. Although neither a negotiating party in the Law of the Sea Conference III nor a contracting party to the Law of the Sea Convention of 1982, Taiwan announced a 12-mile territorial sea and a 200-mile Exclusive Economic Zone on October 8, 1979. On October 2, 1980, the American Institute in Taiwan (AIT) and the Taiwan Coordination Council for North American Affairs (CCNAA)(now known as TECRO, the Taipei Economic and Cultural Representative Office in the United States) signed an agreement on privileges, exemptions, and immunities.[13] They granted a number of traditional diplomatic privileges and immunities to each other.

PRC AND ROC: SPECIAL STATE-TO-STATE RELATIONS?

Objective observation and analysis indicate that there are indeed two states—the PRC on the mainland and the ROC on Taiwan. As discussed above, the ROC remains in existence and maintains a title on Taiwan and a close relationship with the international community, officially or unofficially. Furthermore, the analysis above demonstrates that the ROC on Taiwan is a democratic sovereign state. Since 1949, the PRC regime in Beijing has been the de facto government of the mainland territory, and the ROC regime in Taipei has been the de facto government of Taiwan. The existence in reality of two separate states across the Taiwan Strait seems difficult to deny.

As to the relationship between Taiwan and China, Taiwan admits the existence of two Chinese states: Both are de facto and de jure states controlling their own territories, but neither is the legal government representing both mainland China and Taiwan. Taiwan's "one China, two political entities" policy is designed to bypass the argument over sovereignty—over which is the legitimate government for all China. Also in 1993, Taiwan developed the "two Chinas in transition" expression to address cross-strait relations. While upholding the ultimate goal of reunification, the policy implicitly admits the existence of two Chinese states. This "two Chinas in transition" policy was presented at the APEC (Asia-Pacific Economic Cooperation) press meeting in Seattle on November 20, 1993. There, in response to Beijing's public claims of sovereignty over the island, Taipei's economic minister P. K. Chiang announced that "the ROC government is now pursuing a 'transitional' 'two Chinas policy' and that there are now two sovereign nations across the Taiwan Strait."[14] This "two Chinas in transition" policy also summarized the reality—the long existence of two political entities divided as a result of civil war—without changing the ROC's ultimate goal of unifying China.

The latest remark was in July 1999 when President Lee Teng-hui was asked by a *Deutsche Welle* radio interviewer to comment on China's description of Taiwan as a renegade province. Lee pointed out that "Taiwan has an elected, democratic government" and the definition of the cross-strait relationship is "at least a special state-to-state relationship." President Lee also mentioned that "under such special state-to-state relations, there is no longer any need to declare Taiwan independence" and urged China to "proceed with democratic reforms at an early date to create better conditions for democratic reunification with Taiwan."[15] Beijing has once more accused President Lee of embarking on a quest for Taiwan's independence, which could provoke a Chinese military attack. Subsequent statements by President Lee and other Taiwan officials stress that Taiwan had not abandoned unification as its ultimate goal and that the new remark was only a modest and logical extension of a previous position.

One analyst argues that President Lee's remark reflects growing frustration with Beijing's refusal to accord Taiwan a politically equal position in the cross-strait talks.[16] Beijing fails to understand that Taiwan's democratization in recent years has changed its state structure and mainland policy. A libertarian-civic Taiwan society driven by popular support demands more equal treatment in cross-strait relations and more breathing space in the international community.[17] Taipei argues that

> Beijing has denigrated the ROC as a local government through its hegemonistic one-China principle. It downgraded the ROC in cross-strait exchanges, and appropriated the "one-China principle" as the premise for all cross-strait negotiations, in order to force us to gradually acquiesce to the "one country, two systems" formula.[18]

For Taipei therefore "one China" is something for the future, a *democratic* union with a mainland China that is far different from that of today. For now, Taipei's insistence that the current cross-strait situation is a "special state-to-state relation" is designed to guarantee that cross-strait dialogues and exchanges are conducted on a basis of equality.[19]

Taipei has issued a new official terminology to describe its relations with mainland China as "*one nation, two states.*" The articulation of the relationship is indeed one step away from the previous policy of "one China, two political entities." The major difference between these two descriptions is the replacement of "one China" by "one nation." Taipei reasons that Beijing uses the term "one China" to promote the PRC as the superior sovereign entity and to isolate Taiwan further.[20] In essence, these remarks about "one nation, two states," "two Chinas in transition," or "special state-to-state relations" represent not only policy changes toward cross-strait relations but also strategies to cope with the legal and political dilemma posed by Beijing's "one China" rhetoric.

Legally speaking, when President Lee addressed the cross-strait relationship as a "special state-to-state" relationship, he accurately described current relations between China and Taiwan. On the one hand, Taiwan is a state, although an isolated democracy. On the other hand, the relationship between Taiwan and China is a special state-to-state relationship— a unique situation, a special relationship that has never arisen before, that is different from the two Germanys and the two Koreas. Taiwan and China share the same cultural heritage and historical ties and could achieve the common goal of integration in the future. The Taiwan government's position on President Lee's remark argues that

> [t]his practical and forward-looking view fully voiced the aspira-
> tions of the twenty-two million people in Taiwan. It is designed to
> lay a foundation of parity for the two sides, to elevate the level of
> dialogue, to build a mechanism for democratic and peaceful cross-
> strait interactions, and to usher in a new era of cross-strait rela-
> tions.[21]

CONCLUSION

I have examined Taiwan's legal status and relations with mainland China in light of current political and legal facts and reality. In addition to traditional conditions of statehood, I have proposed a framework for a new approach to democratic sovereignty, internal and external, that determines a political entity's international legal status and its legal personality and capacity.

In addressing relations between China and Taiwan, I have concluded that the PRC and the ROC are, in political and legal reality, two separate states with a unique and special relationship. Many countries fail to understand this important structural change in Taiwan and its relations with China, that is, that Taiwan is now a democracy. Taiwan is a democratic political community with its own constitution and final control of legal jurisdiction. Taiwan is not part of the PRC, nor is it part of the "China" defined by the PRC and other states. Most states disregard the reality that a democratic sovereign state exists on Taiwan, denying Taiwan the rights to liberty, participation, and self-respect of full political participation in the international arena.

Notes

1. According to the general opinion of international lawyers and the Montevideo Convention on Rights and Duties of States, article 1.

2. See Mark S. Zaid, "Taiwan: It Looks Like It, It Acts Like It, But Is It a State? The Ability to Achieve a Dream through Membership in International Organizations," *New England Law Review* 32 (Spring 1998): 805–818.

3. Louis Henkin, Richard C. Pugh, Oscar Schachter, and Hans Smit, *International Law: Cases and Materials*, 2d ed. (St. Paul, Minn.: West Publishing Co., 1987), 278.

4. Constitutive rules can be understood as the basic concepts and relatively unchanging practices that create and define new forms of behavior. See David Dessler, "What's at Stake in the Agent-Structure Debate?" *International Organization* 43 (Summer 1989): 455.

5. See Samuel M. Makinda, "The United Nations and State Sovereignty: Mechanism for Managing International Security," *Australian Journal of Political Science* 33, no. 1 (March 1998): 101–115.

6. Rebecca M. M. Wallance, *International Law* (London: Sweet & Maxwell, 1992), 107.

7. Ingrid Delupis, *International Law and the Independent State* (New York: Crane, Russak Co., 1974), 5.

8. James Crawford, *The Creation of States in International Law* (Oxford: Oxford University Press, 1990), 71.

9. See Lu Ya-li, "Political Developments in the Republic of China," in *Democracy and Development in East Asia: Taiwan, South Korea, and the Philippines*, ed. Thomas W. Robinson (Washington, D.C.: American Enterprise Institute, 1991), 35–48.

10. See Bruce J. Dickson, "China's Democratization and the Taiwan Experience," *Asian Survey* 38, no. 4 (April 1998): 349–364.

11. See Hung-mao Tien and Yun-han Chu, "Building Democratic Institutions in Taiwan," *China Quarterly* 148 (December 1996), 1103–1132.

12. In addition, the Legislative Yuan is responsible for deciding the statutory bills regarding national policies. See Chien-Kuo Pang, *The State and Economic Transformation: The Taiwan Case* (New York: Garland Publishing, 1992), 50–76.

13. The AIT and TECRO are the de facto embassies established by the Taiwan Relations Act after the U.S. government withdrew its recognition of Taipei.

14. The statement was a rebuttal to the PRC president Jiang Jemin's comment that Taiwan was only a province of the PRC. See *China Times*, November 22, 1993, p. 1 (in Chinese).

15. "Taiwan Redefines China Relations," The Associated Press, July 10, 1999, at the Web site of Taiwan Security Research <taiwansecurity.org/AP/AP-990710.htm>.

16. Ralph A. Cossa, "Cross-Straits Relations: Now What?" Pacnet 28, July 16, 1999.

17. For more discussion on Taiwan's democratization and cross-strait relations, see Timothy Ka-ying Wong, "The Impact of State Development in Taiwan on Cross-Strait Relations," *Asian Perspective* 21, no. 1 (Spring–Summer 1997), 171–212.

18. "Parity, Peace and Win-Win: The Republic of China's Position on the 'Special State-to-State Relationship,'" Mainland Affairs Council, Executive Yuan, Republic of China, August 1, 1999.

19. "Taiwan Sees 'One China' as Democratic Ideal," Reuters, July 20, 1999, at the Web site of Taiwan Security Research <taiwansecurity.org/Reu/Reu-990720.htm>.

20. "'One Nation, Two States'—Taiwan Clarifies Chinese Relations," The Associated Press, July 15, 1999, at the Web site of Taiwan Security Research <taiwansecurity.org/AP/AP-990715.htm>.

21. "Parity, Peace and Win-Win: The Republic of China's Position on the 'Special State-to-State Relationship.'"

PART THREE

ECONOMIC DEPENDENCIES AND INTERDEPENDENCIES

CHAPTER SEVEN

LIKE LIPS AND TEETH: ECONOMIC SCENARIOS OF CROSS-STRAIT RELATIONS

Gary H. Jefferson

PETER CHEN OF TAIWAN'S NATIONAL SECURITY COUNCIL sums up the prevailing view of mainland-Taiwan relations: "Economically, we're moving closer and closer, but as far as values and political systems are concerned, we're moving farther and farther apart . . . .. Here lies the dilemma."[1]

Here I have formulated a perspective on this growing economic integration and political disintegration. The perspective evolves from a model of economic relations between mainland China and Taiwan, examines the model's implications for the political dimension of this relationship, and sketches possible future scenarios.

The central conclusion is that, given trends in the global electronics industry on which Taiwan's prosperity depends, the continuation of this prosperity will require political accommodation with the mainland. It is not possible to sustain the current condition of economic integration and political disintegration.

QUALITY LADDER: CONCEPTUAL FRAMEWORK

Raymond Vernon, Paul Krugman, and Gene Grossman and Elhanan Helpman have developed successively sophisticated models of international product cycles and quality ladders that focus on interactions between innovative firms in the "north" and imitators in the "south."[2] In the Grossman and Helpman model, northern firms with high-tech and high-cost manufacturing operations focus on product innovation. Southern firms, with lower production costs, can capture markets from northern rivals by replicating northern products. The north retaliates with fresh rounds of innovation. Rivalry among different types of producers leads to an ongoing evolution of product characteristics, while the locus of manufacturing activity may shift back and forth between firms located in the industrial north and those in the developing south.

The essential nature of China's industrial reform process can be explained by extending these international-quality-ladder models along two dimensions. First, China's domestic industry embodies its own hierarchy of firms that generates domestic versions of the rivalries, pressures, and flows associated with global product cycles. In the early 1990s, a hierarchy placed foreign-invested firms on top of the ladder, followed by larger state-owned enterprises, smaller state-owned enterprises, and urban collectives, township and village enterprises, and privately owned firms.

These ownership types represent a technological ladder with respect to the distribution of technicians, new-product quality, exports, and quality-inspection outcomes. Conversely, for the manufacture of standard products with widely available technologies, such as apparel, toys, and household electronic goods, cost advantages tend to run in the opposite direction of technological capabilities, particularly with respect to labor and overhead.

The ladder concept extends along a second dimension: the idea of a quality ladder in institutions. Successful competition among enterprises occupying different technological and cost rungs of the ladder depends also on effective forms of governance. Enterprises that reform their governance structures enjoy an advantage; those that do not reform face severe pressure to undertake institutional upgrades.

Like the product cycle and quality ladder, this model is dynamic. The dynamism in China's industrial system arises from two principal conditions: the extraordinary technological and institutional diversity of China's enterprise system and the widespread competition that arises from relatively easy entry into the enterprise system and the decentralized control of publicly owned assets that fosters interjurisdictional rivalry.

Competition, both domestic and international, erodes profit margins and the revenue base of the local jurisdictions that enjoy control over many of these enterprises. Falling profits and revenues motivate managers and officials to search for new technologies and the institutional reforms needed to compete effectively. Firms that succeed move up the quality ladder; those that do not succeed go to its lower rungs. From a nationwide perspective, through competition, increasing openness, and an evolving system of law and regulation, new technologies and institutional innovations continually enter the system, both through international markets and China's evolving process of domestic research and development (R&D) and enterprise reform.

This domestic-quality-ladder paradigm provides a useful way to understand China's evolving enterprise system. By the late 1990s, the ladder had probably become less stratified by ownership type than it had been at the beginning of the decade. It is also true that by the late 1990s more sophisticated technology and property-rights markets had emerged to provide a wider range of channels for technology transfer and enterprise restructuring.[3]

TAIWAN'S POSITION ON THE LADDER

Here I seek to fill the lacunae between the global model that Grossman and Helpman formulated for the international arena and the domestic version that Rawski and I developed for the Chinese economy. This critical link focuses on the role that overseas Chinese play in the operation of this quality ladder. In particular, I focus on Taiwan's role in the international quality ladder and its economic relationship with mainland China. Taiwan is not unique in its proximity to China: Hong Kong, Japan, and even the United States play major roles in the technology and capital that they bring to mainland China.

Taiwan may be viewed in a competitive relationship with Hong Kong. With Taiwan's population approximately four times that of

Hong Kong's, Taiwan's presence on the mainland may in the longer run rival or even surpass that of Hong Kong's.

Here we focus on Taiwan's comparative advantage relative to other major players on the mainland.

- *Cultural proximity.* Many residents of Taiwan enjoy family ties with the mainland, with approximately 80 percent tracing their origins to the Fujian province. This cultural and linguistic propinquity effectively lowers the transaction costs of conducting business on the mainland. Only Hong Kong can claim a comparable or superior advantage.

- *Strengths in manufacturing and industrial technology.* Taiwan's robust manufacturing technologies make its economy particularly relevant to the technological dimension of the quality ladder. Taiwan's ability to imitate new products and bring them to market quickly makes it an extremely useful rung up the quality ladder for the mainland, while the mainland's supply of low-cost labor down the ladder is valuable for Taiwan. With its own relatively sophisticated manufacturing capabilities and huge manufacturing investments and trading network in Southeast Asia, far more than Hong Kong's, Taiwan's greatest role on the mainland will be investment and technology transfer to the manufacturing sector.

- *Economic organization focused on small- and medium-size enterprise in the manufacturing sector.* Taiwan's system of small- and medium-size enterprises (SMEs), more highly acclaimed following recent setbacks to Korea's chaebol system of large-size enterprises, provides a useful model for economic reform on the mainland. Among China's 7–8 million industrial enterprises, nearly 20 times that of the United States, all but approximately 25,000 are small-size firms. Taiwan's property-rights market, its equity and venture capital markets, legal and regulatory structures, and R&D system—oriented toward smaller enterprises—offer useful institutional lessons for the reform and consolidation of China's enterprise system.

- *Democratic values and institutions.* By virtue of its special relationship with the mainland, Taiwan's experience of evolving democratic values and structures both intrigues and vexes its mainland counterparts. Although, unlike Hong Kong, Taiwan is not geographically contiguous with the mainland, and therefore does not have a seamless exchange of economic resources, that separation also affords greater protection for Taiwan's evolving political and institutional structure. The ability of Taiwan's institutional arrangements to evolve with a greater measure of independence than those in Hong Kong may ultimately enable Taiwan to facilitate China's creation of the competitive political institutions needed to achieve economic prosperity and full integration into the international system.

One country (region) or another may enjoy one, or even two, of these advantages, but none combines all four advantages as Taiwan does.

RECENT HISTORY OF TAIWAN'S FDI AND TRADE WITH THE MAINLAND

Taiwan came relatively late to the mainland arena. After a 40-year freeze, Taiwan's government in 1987 abolished martial law and lifted the ban on kinship visits to the mainland. Taiwan's economic relations with the mainland quickly took off, overshadowing its trade and FDI (foreign direct investment) in the ASEAN (Association of Southeast Asian Nations) countries.

Trade

In 1997, exports from Taiwan to the mainland and Hong Kong amounted to $26.78 billion. According to Taiwan's statistics, approximately $20 billion of these exports, nearly 17 percent of Taiwan's total exports, were destined for the mainland. Internationally, Taiwan stands third, well behind Japan and very close to the United States, as a supplier of exports to the mainland.[4] In 1997, imports from the mainland had not yet reached $4 billion.

Foreign Direct Investment

Taipei's requirement that companies channel mainland investments through third countries creates uncertainty about the size of the flow. As reported by the *Far Eastern Economic Review*,

> Taipei's Investment Commission says it approved $13.2 billion worth of investments through 1998, but Beijing says Taiwanese firms have remitted a total of $21 billion and independent estimates go as high as $30 billion. Even the lowest of these figures amounts to 43 percent of Taiwan's overseas investment through 1998.[5]

Taiwan's official statistics show that, in 1998, Taiwan investors completed approximately $2 billion of FDI on the mainland. The vast majority of this FDI, $1.8 billion, materialized in the manufacturing sector.[6]

At the end of 1992, Taiwan's cumulative FDI on the mainland revealed a profile different from the rest of the world. Taiwan's FDI in transportation equipment and nonmetallic mineral products was minimal, whereas FDI in plastic products, processed foods, machinery, and miscellaneous products was overrepresented. Although in 1992 Taiwan's FDI in the electrical machinery and apparatus industry represented the largest share of Taiwan's FDI (13.12 percent), it still lagged behind the 15.12 percent share from the rest of the world.[7] But this changed rapidly.

Modeling the shifting comparative advantages of Taiwan and China, Chung concludes that "successive waves of Taiwanese FDI toward the mainland were, more than anything, a manifestation of the changing comparative advantage in production and trade between the two countries."[8] Among the traditional labor-intensive industries that lost trade shares were apparel, plastic products, metal products, and electrical and electronic products. But these were precisely the areas in which Taiwan's FDI to the mainland accelerated during the early and mid-1990s.

Electronics Industry

Taiwan's electronics industry was initiated by an influx of FDI in the 1960s and 1970s from Western and Japanese multinational corporations (MNCs), including RCA, Zenith, and Matsushita.[9] Although investment from these MNCs represented approximately one-quarter of total investment in Taiwan's electronics industry, in the 1970s production from foreign-affiliated ventures accounted for more than 60 percent of electronics exports. By the early 1980s, electronics exports overtook textiles as Taiwan's biggest foreign-exchange earner.

The personal computer (PC) industry, unlike earlier consumer electronics industries, was established in Taiwan largely through indigenous effort. Taiwan's indigenous capabilities in PC manufacture developed from its experience in the manufacture of televisions and calculators and its assembly of audio and visual equipment. These provided a solid foundation for the subsequent development of PC products, including terminals and monitors. The development of a robust manufacturing sector in audiovisual components also attracted many engineers experienced in circuit design and the application of microprocessors. Establishment of a system of research institutes and science parks was also critical in drawing back to Taiwan overseas Chinese with computer backgrounds with the skill and capital needed to set up PC-related businesses.

Taiwan's FDI in the PC Industry

Chung notes that in 1983, just one year after the world's first IBM-compatible PC XT was introduced by Compaq, Acer presented Taiwan's first IBM-compatible PC XT and ignited a subsequent rapid expansion of Taiwan's domestic PC industry.[10]

By the late 1980s, rising labor and land costs were eroding Taiwan's comparative advantage in producing lower-end PC products. Before the mainland became available as an outlet for FDI in the PC industry, Taiwan's FDI flowed principally toward ASEAN countries, especially Malaysia and Thailand, first with the manufacture of keyboards and switch power supplies and later with monitors and motherboards.

Taiwan firms did not deploy large investments to the mainland until 1990, but during the following several years FDI accelerated explosively. By 1993, China's share of Taiwan's offshore production of PC hardware accounted for 34.6 percent, exceeding the shares contributed by Thailand and Malaysia. As shown by Chung, relative to home production, manufacturing operations in the mainland provided Taiwan's producers of PC components savings in unit costs ranging from 8 to 22 percent and savings relative to ASEAN venues of 3 to 8 percent. [11]

By 1995, the electronics sector accounted for 23 percent of Taiwan's manufacturing output and more than 35 percent of its total exports.[12] Total domestic PC-related output grew to an impressive $15.8 billion, 90 percent of which was furnished by Taiwan-owned firms. Together with an offshore production value of $5.4 billion, Taiwan surpassed Germany to become the world's third-largest PC maker. In 1995, Taiwan's major products included desktop and portable PCs, computer monitors, motherboards, keyboards, PC mouse devices, and switch-power-supply units, some of which accounted for half or more of the world's total production.

Taiwan's FDI on the mainland, focused on the electronics sector, continues to drive Taiwan's FDI and much of Taiwan's industrial economy. During the past few years, Taiwan's electronics companies have shifted 29 percent of their computer-related manufacturing to mainland China—and they say that it's only the beginning.

The National Federation of Industries, Taiwan's largest manufacturing association, estimates that one-third of the nearly 30,000 companies licensed to do business on the mainland are electronics companies.[13] According to Taiwan's Investment Commission, among the 144 electronics companies listed on Taiwan's main stock exchange and its over-the-counter market, 26 percent have received approval for mainland investments. Security analysts estimate that at least an equal number are preparing to invest there.[14]

PROBLEMS OF EXIT

Both on the mainland and on Taiwan, obstacles to the exit of low-end products and whole firms threaten to undermine the functioning of the international product ladder. For the mainland, the problem is long-standing, deeply rooted in its enterprise, financial, and social security systems. Arguably, although Taiwan's problem is more subtle, it is potentially as serious, if not more serious, than the mainland's exit problem.

Mainland's Exit Problem

Through the latter half of the 1990s, Chinese industry has been plagued by overcapacity, inventory accumulation, and falling prices. The 1995 industrial census reported that the average utilization rate in Chinese industry stood at just 70 percent, indicating that levels of excess capacity have probably not improved in the face of Asia's financial crisis. But the problem is not just one of short-term aggregate demand, it reflects the chronic proliferation of enterprises that cause most to operate well below their minimum efficiency scale.

In 1998, for example, China's automobile industry produced 1.63 million automobiles. With 123 automobile plants, average production was less than 15,000, only approximately one-twentieth of the minimum efficiency scale of a typical automobile plant. China has 8,000 cement producers versus just 1,500 on average in the rest of the world; 1,570 companies make steel. With state and collective enterprise pursuing a range of social objectives, including employment creation, many are established or sustained without commercial justification. Local governments often subsidize firms to maintain their production even if there is no market for their products.

The Chinese government has initiated a range of measures to reduce the persistence of excess capacity. Some of them appear to be counterproductive, including requiring the manufacturers of 21 key consumer products to set minimum price "floors," prohibiting new investment in 201 product lines, and suspending production in key industries, such as the coordinated two to three week shutdown in the television color-tube industry. To address chronic excess capacity on the mainland, the government is also arranging mergers—"forced marriages"—such as plans for the steel industry to consolidate state-owned enterprises, including loss-making enterprises and small enterprises, to form four large groups that account for 40 percent of national production.

The persistence of excess capacity throughout China's industrial economy reduces returns to FDI. Additionally, by undermining fiscal and financial stability, the channeling of resources to weak enterprises creates the specter of risk. Both make China's industrial economy a less attractive destination for FDI and slow the functioning of the quality ladder.

By giving the appearance of micromanagement, many measures described above raise the flag of central planning. An effective resolution of the excess-capacity problem will require market-mediated solutions based on legal and regulatory measures, including well-functioning bankruptcy laws and capital markets, to facilitate the restructuring of weak enterprises through bankruptcies, mergers, and acquisitions.[15] A more complete social insurance system is needed to facilitate the transition of workers so as to reduce the burden of unemployment, its threat to political stability, and the compulsion of governments at all levels to channel resources to weak enterprises. In the longer term, China may have to allow greater political competition and democratic participation if the elite's political legitimacy is to be widened beyond its current precarious balance on economic growth.

Finally, by reducing protection, both tariffs and subsidies, and enhancing transparency, China's accession to the WTO (World Trade Organization) is important for promoting the trade and FDI needed to enhance the functioning of the quality ladder.

Taiwan's Exit Problem

Critics of Taiwan's accelerating flow of FDI to China draw parallels with Hong Kong's experience, including the migration of its manufacturing to the mainland, a rise in income and wealth disparities, and the reluctance of Hong Kong's businesses to offend China. The discussion below attempts to distinguish between "hollowing out" and political dependence. In fact, just as drawing a line between the economic and the political dimensions of the mainland's exit problem is difficult, Taiwan's exit problem is difficult to demonstrate.

Hollowing out. Chen Po-chih of the Taiwan Institute of Economic Research asserts that, because land and labor on the mainland cannot move, Taiwan's capital, technology, and workforce flow across the border, leading to "a hollowing out of our industry." Chen suggests a suitable degree of policy intervention to avoid following Hong Kong's tracks.[16]

Chang Jung-feng, economics professor at National Taiwan University, adds the following: "The real point of the 'go-slow' policy is listed companies should not use capital from small investors [in Taiwan] or take large amounts of our banking system's capital to invest in the mainland's risky market, especially as Beijing refuses to abandon the use of force against us."[17]

Chen recommends adopting a broader framework requiring that "a certain share of funds raised on the public market by a company be devoted for domestic investment." Moreover, he argues, "we can adopt a case-by-case review system for applications by [mainland] companies to make capital investments in Taiwan and thus display our sincerity for mutually beneficial cross-strait ties."[18]

Taipei prohibits companies from assembling notebook computers on the mainland. Although Acer, which manufacturers laptops and notebooks for IBM, Fujitsu, and Hitachi, puts its notebooks together in Taiwan, it does have a Shanghai subcontractor handle some internal assembly. President of Acer Peripherals, K. Y. Lee, contends that "without our China operations, we couldn't compete with the Japanese."[19] These restrictions threaten to limit the competitiveness and profitability of Taiwan's PC producers.

In addition to these barriers to outflows of PC-related FDI to the mainland, in its annual outlook, the Asian Development Bank notes the following areas of "bureaucratic inertia" that retard both inflows and outflows of resources to and from Taiwan's economy:

- Lengthy approval procedures for business operating licenses;

- Foreign-exchange controls involving tedious reviews of foreign portfolio and FDI flows;

- Restrictions on travel, residence visas, and work permits; and

- A heavy tax burden on income and capital gains of foreign companies (as high at 40 percent compared with Hong Kong's 16.5 percent).[20]

Political dependence. Critics also worry that the flood of Taiwan investment to the mainland will make Taipei economically dependent on the mainland, undermining its de facto political independence.

Those arguing for a go-slow approach toward liberalizing Taiwan's economic relationship with the mainland emphasize that the chief risk is that, as its mainland stakes grow, Taiwan industry will push Taipei to soften its stand toward Beijing.[21] Opponents note that already Taiwan companies have forced Taipei to allow limited shipping links with the mainland as well as commercial flights that stop in Macao merely to change flight numbers. In 1994, major PC producers in Taiwan, led by Acer, persuaded the Taiwan government to loosen restrictions on the mainland's assembling of Pentium processors, at that time the most powerful chips available for production in Taiwan.

Taipei would have preferred to use such linkages as bargaining chips to wring political concessions from Beijing.

Although there may be sound political reasons for blocking its exit passage, the policy carries an economic cost. If the productions of products that lie lower down the quality ladder are not deployed to lower-cost locations, the misallocation of scarce resources, including engineers and capital, will slow the process of internal adjustment and depress returns to Taiwan's factors of production.

In principle, both the mainland and Taiwan are committed to setting in place policies to support the dynamic restructuring of their domestic industrial economies. Both embrace the principles of reform: the mainland's "opening up to the outside world" and Taiwan's "fostering internal economic dynamism." But the presence of reform ideology does not guarantee the desired results in a timely manner.

TAIWAN AT A CROSSROADS:
WILL IT BE BUMPED OFF THE LADDER?

Surveying Taiwan's 1995 performance, Chung has suggested that "Taiwan's PC industry [is] at the crossroads." He noted that "downstream PC producers [i.e., Taiwan firms] still imported 84 percent of the required information ICs [integrated circuits], 85 percent of the LCDs [liquid-crystal displays], and 99 percent of the CPUs [central processing units]."[22] In that year the five largest dynamic RAM (DRAM) suppliers were all foreign MNCs. As Chung summarizes,

> Taiwan's PC industry is at a fork in the road. Having established itself as a credible manufacturer of PC hardware, it now faces the difficult choice of continuing exploiting its manufacturing capabilities—but increasingly at another geographic location—or making an entry into new product areas characterized by high risk and uncertainty.[23]

Specifically, Taiwan faces two challenges: excessive reliance on imports of upstream components and horizontal integration of the electronics industry. As Dieter Ernst writes,

> Despite all of its achievements, Taiwan's electronics industry is still based on a weak foundation. For most of the key components that determine the price and the performance features of its major export products, Taiwan continues to rely heavily on imports, particularly from Japan.[24]

Ernst notes Taiwan's particular dependence on cathode-ray tubes and display panels. "For this industry," Ernst writes with prescience, "the ability to purchase display panels in the necessary quantities, at the right time and at a reasonable price, will decide its competitive success."[25]

Such an example of Taiwan's vulnerability to the timely supply of key components has recently materialized.[26] Acer and other Taiwan PC makers are frustrated by their dependence on imports from Japan and South Korea for key components, most notably flat panel monitors (TFT-LCDs [thin-film-transistor liquid-crystal displays]). These state-of-the art devices account for approximately one-third of a notebook PC's production costs. Because of the newness, robust demand, and short supply of these components, Taiwan computer firms suffer from lower margins and production disruptions while Japanese and South Korean firms enjoy windfall profits.

With licensed know-how from IBM Japan and a $600 million investment, Acer has set out to produce its own TFT-LCDs. Acer acknowledges the risks in this investment, although the Taiwan company believes it can use low-cost manufacturers in Taiwan and offshore locations, notably the mainland, to compete with its South Korean rivals. In the meantime, South Korean makers are linking with foreign partners to move quickly to the next generation of larger flat panel monitors.

This example underscores the implications for its economy of Taiwan's efforts to move upstream. The large-scale technological, capital, and marketing requirements for moving upstream require a fundamental realtering of Taiwan's SME corporate structure. To move upstream, Taiwan must substantially expand the scale of a number of its leading firms, at the expense of the SME sector. The island's economy will also have to be even more specialized than it is now in electronics and the PC and IC industries.

Even if Taiwan succeeds in its continued timely imitation of critical PC components, it faces a more complex problem. The growing emphasis on integrated, user-friendly applications is rapidly bringing a convergence between 3-C (computer, communications, and consumer electronics) products while redirecting the global PC market toward a multimedia and network-centered stage. The problem, Chung points out, is that effective entry into this horizontally integrated market requires huge amounts of R&D. Moreover U.S. and Japanese MNCs hold patents over much of this emerging technological landscape, which can thwart even well-financed efforts by Taiwan to break into these new innovation frontiers.

Taiwan may hope to maintain its timely imitation of strategic PC components, combined with low-cost offshore production, or move up the ladder with an emphasis on innovation in a field with increasingly integrated technologies. But the island's economy will have to complement its indigenous resources with supplies of highly mobile capital and technical labor.

Vertical Integration of Manufacturing

During the past decade, Motorola, Philips, IBM, Apple, Hewlett Packard, Intel, and other U.S. and Japanese electronics giants have established research and manufacturing types of facilities on the mainland. Microsoft recently announced plans to establish a joint R&D facility at Beijing's Haidian technology park.

This is the second challenge to Taiwan's PC industry. By integrating downstream into China's manufacturing system, U.S. and Japanese MNCs are establishing the possibility of eliminating the middle man (i.e., Taiwan). Successful vertical integration between the top and bottom rungs of the product ladder will allow the major innovators to capture rents from low-cost production on the mainland that Taiwanese producers have enjoyed by virtue of their low transaction costs.

Taiwan's Choices

In response to these trends in the computer sector, Taiwanese producers face two possibilities.

The first is to move upstream. Rather than producing for brand-name manufacturers, Taiwan can attempt to create firms able to undertake the huge investments in R&D and marketing needed to create their own brands. This appears to be one avenue, albeit a risky one, for Taiwan's PC producers. The payoff is the ability to capture rents from patented innovations and brand-name products.

A second is to follow the initiative of U.S. and Japanese MNCs to integrate vertically with mainland suppliers. The rents that Taiwan's manufacturers capture from FDI on the mainland accrue from the lower transaction costs that they enjoy owing to Taiwan's cultural and geographic proximity to the mainland. As U.S. MNCs attempt to expand on the mainland and erode the rents secured by Taiwan suppliers, Taiwan will have to reduce further transaction costs by further normalizing relations with the mainland, including direct transportation, communications, and banking. Taiwan's producers can employ these reductions in transaction costs to move into more remote, lower-cost regions of China, away from the higher-cost centers where U.S. and Japanese MNCs are investing.

Either initiative reinforces Taiwan's position on the quality ladder. The best solution may be to pursue both initiatives—reducing transactions costs of FDI deployed to the mainland and moving up the quality ladder—so as to compete with U.S. and Japanese MNCs in bringing new technologies and products directly to the mainland and also to secure rents from Taiwan-owned patents and brand names.

As Acer's move into TFT-LCD production demonstrates, initiative both up and down the ladder may be needed for Taiwan to retain successfully its niche on the global quality ladder. To move successfully into the LCD market, Taiwan must both mobilize the resource commitments necessary to challenge upstream innovators and producers and reduce the transaction costs of sourcing FDI to the mainland to cut costs and extend the life of earlier generations of evolving product lines.

INSTITUTIONAL AND POLITICAL IMPLICATIONS

As all economies are, Taiwan's international commercial relations and its economic prosperity are founded on political stability. Over the past two decades, the one-China policy and the Taiwan Relations Act have been a framework for maintaining stability and prosperity, not only in Taiwan but also throughout the region. These agreements created the political framework that has sustained the quality ladder that links Taiwan to the global electronics industry and facilitates cross-strait trade and investment in this industry.

Arguably, Taipei has more at stake than Beijing in maintaining a stable, constructive political relationship. Failure to do so will interfere with the normalization of Taiwan's relations with the mainland, including establishment of the transportation and communications needed to reduce the transaction costs of Taiwan's FDI on the mainland.

If the competitive advantage enjoyed by Taiwan's mainland operations weakens, Taiwan will have to move all the more aggressively into the highly competitive and costly innovation arenas at higher rungs of the ladder.

This moving-up strategy will also require strategic foreign joint ventures and huge commitments of foreign capital. Unstable mainland-Taiwan relations will make it more difficult for Taiwan to establish foreign alliances and attract the highly mobile capital necessary to break successfully into the U.S. and Japanese circle of producers.

In a recent survey 56 percent of Asian executives reported that rising cross-strait tension would not affect their inclinations to invest in Taiwan, whereas 39 percent said that they are now less likely to invest in Taiwan.[27] Those who express willingness to invest in an environment of rising tensions may do so only for the benefit of higher returns, which implies diminished returns for their Taiwan partners.

To achieve one or both prongs of the strategy of maintaining or expanding Taiwan's position on the quality ladder, Taipei may also have to supplement its own skilled workforce with international supplies of scientists, engineers, and business people. Hong Kong during the 1990s became a mecca for PRC Chinese with freshly minted degrees in business, economics, and finance from the United States. In a similar way, Taiwan's position on the global ladder could be considerably enhanced by young Chinese—from both the PRC and overseas—bringing their business and engineering skills to Taiwan.

CONCLUSIONS AND ISSUES

In the long run, China can be a regional growth engine but only as long as continuing liberalization allows for the exit of antiquated products and manufacturing processes. This continued restructuring and opening, facilitated by membership in the WTO, are needed to sustain acceptable rates of return of foreign investment in the mainland.

Likewise, for the mainland-Taiwan link along the quality ladder to strengthen and grow, Taiwan will need to sustain its effort at the top and bottom of its ladder niche. Like China, Taiwan will have to keep open its exit channels to allow competitive conditions to drive Taipei technology, capital, and management know-how to low-cost regions on the mainland. At the upper end, Taiwan will be well served by expanding its R&D and marketing capabilities, although this will likely require a substantial enlargement of Taiwan's corporate scale and resource base.

For Taiwan not to move in these directions risks being bumped off the PC and IC quality ladder, as U.S. and Japanese electronic MNCs make their own mainland plays. Through direct backward integration, these established MNCs are acquiring the potential to develop sophisticated networks of research, manufacture, and marketing on the mainland that can match, then bypass, Taiwan's capabilities.

Against the backdrop of changes in the global PC industry, particularly the way in which the major players are lining up to expand their operations in mainland China, political détente between Taiwan and the mainland is critical to preserving and expanding their relationship on the quality ladder. Continued political instability will erode the ability of Taiwan's producers to reduce further the transaction costs of mainland-directed FDI; it will also motivate major MNCs and foreign capital to stay away. In these conditions, it is unlikely that continued economic integration and political disintegration can be sustained.

Taiwan's economic vulnerability to political instability provides the mainland with a strategic policy instrument. China can use the instrument to create instability to punish unwanted initiatives from Taiwan that weaken the one-China policy. A more troubling scenario is one in which the mainland believes that, because it will lead to independence, the status quo is not acceptable. In this scenario, to erode Taiwan's position on the product ladder and by extension its economic prosperity, the mainland may seek to foster continuing instability in cross-strait political relations.

From the perspective of achieving greater economic prosperity on both sides of the strait, particularly from the perspective of the international product ladder, both the mainland and Taiwan have an interest in establishing interim, if not permanent, arrangements for reducing political tensions.

Notes

1. "Dangerous Liaisons," *Far Eastern Economic Review*, March 25, 1999 (interactive edition).

2. Raymond Vernon, "Intentional Investment and International Trade in the Product Cycle," *Quarterly Journal of Economics* 80, no. 2 (1966): 190–207. Paul Krugman, "A Model of Innovation, Technology Transfer, and the World Distribution of Income," *Journal of Political Economy* 87 (1979): 253–266. Gene M. Grossman and Elhanan Helpman, "Quality Ladders and Product Cycles," *Quarterly Journal of Economics* 106 (1991): 557–586.

3. Gary H. Jefferson and Thomas G. Rawski, "How Industrial Reform Worked in China: The Role of Innovation, Competition, and Property Rights," *Proceedings of the World Bank Annual Conference on Development Economics, 1994* (1995), 129–170. Albert G. Z. Hu and Gary H. Jefferson, "China's National Innovation System," prepared for the workshop on Innovation and Technology Transfer in Chinese Industry, Graduate School of International Economics and Finance, Brandeis University, October 8, 9, 1999.

4. Taiwan (ROC) Statistics Bureau, April 4, 1999 <140.129.146.192/dgbas 03/bs8mainland/1998-d.htm>.

5. "Dangerous Liaisons," *Far Eastern Economic Review*.

6. Taiwan (ROC) Statistics Bureau, April 4, 1999.

7. See Table 6-2 on page 169 in Chin Chung, "Division of Labor Across the Taiwan Strait: Macro Overview and Analysis of the Electronics Industry," in *China Circle: Economics and Technology in the PRC, Taiwan, and Hong Kong*, ed. Barry Naughton (Washington, D.C.: Brookings, 1997), 164–209.

8. Ibid., 170.

9. Much of the description here is drawn from Chin Chung's excellent review of the development of China's electronics and PC industries from 1980 through 1995.

10. Chin Chung, "Division of Labor across the Taiwan Strait."

11. Ibid., Table 6-11.

12. Ibid., 181.

13. "Dangerous Liaisons," *Far Eastern Economic Review*.

14. Ibid.

15. Gary H. Jefferson and Thomas G. Rawski, "China's Emerging Property Rights Market," working paper no. 34, Graduate School of International Economics and Finance, Brandeis University, Waltham, Mass., 1999.

16. "Dangerous Liaisons," *Far Eastern Economic Review*.

17. Ibid.

18. "Go-Slow Policy Creator Urges Change," *South China Morning Post,* September 8, 1999 (archive search).

19. Ibid.

20. Asian Development Bank, *Asian Development Outlook, 1997 and 1998* (New York: Oxford University Press, 1997).

21. "Dangerous Liaisons," *Far Eastern Economic Review.*

22. Chin Chung, "Division of Labor across the Taiwan Strait," 194.

23. Ibid., 196.

24. Dieter Ernst, "Partners for the China Circle? The East Asian Production Networks of Japanese Electronics Industries," in *China Circle: Economics and Technology in the PRC, Taiwan, and Hong Kong*, ed. Barry Naughton (Washington, D.C.: Brookings, 1997), 210–253.

25. Ibid., 241.

26. "Headlong Plunge," *Far Eastern Economic Review*, June 10, 1999 (interactive edition).

27. "Asian Executive's Poll," *Far Eastern Economic Review,* August 5, 1999 (interactive edition).

CHAPTER EIGHT

MAINLAND CHINA AND TAIWAN'S WTO ENTRY: CROSS-STRAIT ECONOMIC AND TRADE PROSPECTS
Wang Jianmin

THE ENTRY OF BOTH MAINLAND CHINA AND TAIWAN into the WTO (World Trade Organization) is an important event in the history of cross-strait economic and trade relations at the turn of the century. It is hoped that the two sides will enter the WTO one after the other or reach a framework on their entry. Their possible entry into the WTO will not only provide new opportunities for economic development. It will also promote overall cross-strait economic and trade relations; accelerate direct postal, commercial, and communication links; and deepen economic integration in the greater China region.

WTO PROSPECTS AND THEIR SIGNIFICANCE

The entry of the two sides into the WTO is consistent with current trends. Since reform and opening-up began in 1978, China's economic system is being transformed into a market economy and gradually perfected into a socialist market economic system with Chinese characteristics. This facilitates China's economic integration with the world economy.

China has seen significant economic achievements during this 20-year development. In 1998, China's GDP (gross domestic product) amounted to $960.9 billion, ranking seventh in the world. Foreign two-way trade has grown rapidly, amounting to $324 billion, ranking eleventh in the world. China has been excluded from GATT (General

Agreement on Tariffs and Trade) and the WTO despite a decade of Chinese effort to enter because Western countries ignore the basic fact that China remains a developing country. This situation is unfavorable not only to China's economic development but also to Western economic interests, especially in shaping a new world trade order. In the new international economic and political situation, through continual Sino-U.S. efforts, the negotiations saw a substantive breakthrough in early 1999, reducing the major barrier to China's entry. Although Sino-U.S. relations suffered a serious setback after the PRC embassy bombing in Belgrade and China's WTO entry met new difficulties, China still hopes to enter the WTO in early 2000.

China's WTO entry will be a short-term shock and a negative impact on some industries; agriculture; and the automobile, telecommunications, and financial sectors. Market competition will become more fierce, but opportunities will outweigh challenges. China will enter the twenty-first century's new international economic order as an initiatory member state. According to a Goldman-Sachs Asian Department simulation, after China enters the WTO, by 2005, lowered tariffs and various lifted restrictions will contribute a 0.5–0.6 percentage point to Chinese GDP. Trade volume will increase from $324 billion in 1998 to $600 billion. Foreign direct investment will increase from $45 billion to $100 billion as transnational corporations throng to China. Although calculations may vary, the significance of China's WTO entry is self-evident.

The mainland's entry will facilitate Taiwan's entry as an independent tariff region. Taiwan is also an important world trade entity with a 1998 trade volume of $215.4 billion, ranking 14th in the world. It is expected that Taiwan will enter after the mainland as the Taiwan, Penghu, Jinmen, and Matsu Tariff Region. Because Taiwan has many years of experience with economic liberalization and internationalization, its market is more open; its economy will therefore face less shock than that of the mainland.

On this matter, the mainland and Taiwan have achieved some understanding and implicit agreement. The mainland agrees with Taiwan's WTO entry as an independent tariff region after the mainland's entry. Taiwan watched with expectant anticipation the mainland's major progress toward WTO admission in 1999. This attitude created a benign environment for economic relations and economic cooperation between the two sides. But Lee Teng-hui's state-to-state theory undercut cross-strait relations and cast a shadow on cross-strait economic and trade relations.

If China fails to enter the WTO this year because of dramatic changes in the international political, economic, and security environment, it will lose a key opportunity to participate in the new international trade order. Such would be detrimental both to China's modernization drive and economic development and the establishment of the new world trade order. Although China's reform and opening-up policy will not waver, its degree and plan for opening-up will require adjustment. Some commitments may not be fulfilled on time, and U.S. and other Western business interests in China may suffer. Taiwan's WTO entry may also be delayed. Its chances of entering the WTO before the mainland are slim.

TAIWAN'S MAINLAND ECONOMIC RELATIONS AND TRADE: POLICIES AND OPTIONS

The entry of the two sides into the WTO may put pressure on Taiwan to relax its restrictive economic and trade policies toward the mainland.

First, after entering the WTO, Taiwan must decide whether to apply the "exclusion clause" to the mainland. If not, Taiwan will need to adjust its policies and lift some restrictions on cross-strait economic intercourse. Taiwan has not yet announced whether it will apply the clause, claiming such "should be decided on whether our industrial interests will be at stake." Judging from the current situation, Taiwan will probably not apply this clause and will make WTO entry its priority. Taiwan could still restrict cross-strait trade through antidumping, antisubsidy, or exercising the security clause after entering the WTO.

Second, WTO entry may force Taiwan to abandon or revise any mainland economic and trade policies inconsistent with WTO principles of nondiscrimination, national treatment, most-favored-nation treatment, tariff protection, transparency, or fair trade. Taiwan's policymakers are reviewing and debating the cross-strait economic and trade implications of Taiwan's WTO entry. Today, as economies become increasingly global, business interests become the priority, and it is impossible for Taiwan authorities to block cross-strait economic intercourse and capital flow. Taiwan would benefit from lifting all unproductive restrictions, from following historical trends, and from creating a win-win situation for both sides.

Last, the two sides entering the WTO will require Taiwan to reconsider its current policy of "avoiding hastiness and exercising restraint" regarding mainland trade and investment. Taiwan will not abandon this policy, at least in Lee Teng-hui's tenure. All-round direct communications are still some time away. Internal and external pressures and economic interests will cause Taiwan gradually to open cross-strait economic and trade exchange.

MAINLAND AND TAIWAN WTO ENTRY: IMPLICATIONS FOR CROSS-STRAIT ECONOMIC AND TRADE RELATIONS

The entry of the two sides into the WTO has great significance for cross-strait trade and investment, including a changing investment structure, direct communications, and economic integration of greater China.

Facilitating Cross-Strait Trade and Investment

Cross-strait trade, which has developed significantly in the past 20 years, constitutes an important component in cross-strait economic relations. By June 1999, total cross-strait trade reached $147.6 billion. But the full potential has not been brought into play. Taiwan's restrictive policies still impede cross-strait trade. After the mainland and Taiwan enter the WTO, markets on both sides will be more open, mutual import tariffs will be reduced, nontariff imports will be less closely controlled, and cross-strait trade volume will increase. All this will help Taiwan reverse the slide after Asia's financial crisis, possibly even sparking new growth.

First, Taiwan's exports to the mainland will see new growth. The mainland's tariff cuts and market liberalization will promote Taiwan's exports to the mainland. The mainland's continuing economic development after it enters the WTO and expanding economies of scale will fuel import needs, facilitating Taiwan's exports to the mainland. The mainland's policy of expanding domestic demand is also helpful in this regard. In 1999, Taiwan's exports to the mainland grew rapidly. According to Taiwan's statistics, exports to the mainland reached $8.15 billion from January through May 1999, with an annual growth rate of 9.8 percent, a new four-year high.

Second, the mainland's export potential to Taiwan is equally large. The mainland's exports to Taiwan currently amount to around $4 billion, which is not in proportion to the $100 billion of Taiwan's annual total imports. If Taiwan were to allow more of the mainland's imports, the mainland's exports to Taiwan could grow significantly. Taipei's financial authorities are expected to complete revision of Taiwan's import tariff laws, in a way favorable to the mainland's exports to Taiwan. Meanwhile, under the new trade rules after the mainland enters the WTO, Taiwan-invested enterprises on the mainland can sell more products back to Taiwan.

Third, Taiwan businesses are eager to seize the opportunities brought by European and U.S. markets opening to the mainland. Because the mainland will enter the WTO as a developing country, it will enjoy unconditional most-favored-nation treatment of all signatory states and may also enjoy general preferential tariff treatment. Restrictions on and discrimination toward the mainland's products from Western countries will decrease. The above factors can ensure the mainland's export expansion, which also favors export of Taiwan-invested enterprises. Cuts in the mainland's import tariff can reduce the import costs of raw material and parts for Taiwan's enterprises, thus strengthening their export competitive edge. Many of Taiwan's entrepreneurs are optimistic regarding this point.

But cross-strait trade will remain indirect until cross-strait relations achieve major breakthroughs.

Changing Structure of Taiwan's Mainland Investments

New trends in Taiwan's investment on the mainland may include the following:

- Taiwan's business will expand into the mainland's vast interior market. After the mainland enters the WTO, the interior market will open, the investment environment and the legal system will improve, and investment policies will become more transparent. Thus more Taiwan businesses will focus on China's interior market. After the PRC enters the WTO, tariff cuts will lower prices on many products and stimulate domestic consumption, especially rural consumption—all good news for Taiwan business.

- Telecommunications, tourism, foreign trade, wholesaling and retailing, and services will be the sectors of choice for Taiwan businesses in the twenty-first century. In these areas, Taiwan is more mature than the mainland. Although the mainland has not opened its commercial wholesale and retail markets to Taiwan, some cooperation exists. Taiwan has built some beachheads on the mainland and has developed them remarkably. As mainland living standards have improved, domestic and overseas sightseeing have become the mainland's fast-growing industries, potentially drawing Taiwan investment. The mainland is ready to open its promising and profitable telecommunications market, facilitating Taiwan investments and cross-strait telecommunications cooperation. Legal services, accounting services, and advertising will also attract Taiwan investment.

- High-tech industries will be leading forces in the future economy, a new area of cross-strait economic cooperation. Taiwan has strong science and technology industries but is excessively concentrated in some areas of the electrical and information industries, with insufficient science and technology human resources. The mainland has abundant science and technology human resources and strong R&D (research and development) capabilities. In addition, the mainland has promised to remove all tariffs on semiconductor, computer, telecommunications facilities, and other science and technology products before

2005 and to abandon the requirements that foreign-invested high-tech enterprises transfer technology and export quotas to the mainland. All this should benefit Taiwan businesses that are adept at information technology. The mainland's high-tech power and potential can draw Taiwan's R&D and production bases onto the mainland.

- Securities and insurance are also new investment areas for Taiwan businesses. The mainland's insurance industry is gradually opening to Taiwan and foreign businesses. By early 1999, foreign-invested financial institutions and enterprises had opened more than 190 business institutions on the mainland with total assets of $36 billion. The mainland has promised to allow foreign-owned banks to run retail business, foreign-invested banks to run renminbi business, and foreign insurance companies to hold 50 percent shares. At the moment, Taiwan investment on the mainland in these areas is quite limited, but Taiwan's financial institutions in Hong Kong can be a bridge to the mainland's insurance industry.

- Taiwan business investment and cooperation in automobile, chemical, petroleum, cement, environment protection, construction, and agriculture may see future development.

Advancing Direct Communications

After the mainland enters the WTO, Taiwan will enter as the Taiwan, Penghu, Jinmen, and Matsu Tariff Region, permitting the two WTO members to conduct economics and trade in a new regulatory framework. Because Taiwan represents an independent tariff region, cross-strait economics and trade still constitute a special relationship in a unified country, that is, economics and trade between China and its independent tariff region, which is not equal to an economics and trade relationship between WTO members. In the twenty-first century, the two sides should establish a new cross-strait economics and trade relationship within the WTO basic framework.

Direct communications are needed to establish a new cross-strait economics and trade framework and realize economic integration.

The entry of the two sides into the WTO makes possible direct communications as a bridge for cross-strait economic integration, which is also important for Taiwan's economic development in the twenty-first century.

The experience of the past 20 years proves that direct communications will foster Taiwan's economy and cross-strait economic and trade development. This is the common wish of those on both sides of the strait. Taiwan should use this opportunity for a gradual realization of direct communications. If not, Taiwan will lose new business opportunities.

Accelerating Cross-Strait Economic Integration

The entry into WTO by the mainland and Taiwan will accelerate an inevitable process of cross-strait economic integration. In the past 20 years, cross-strait economic contact and integration have advanced in an informal, spontaneous way. In the twenty-first century, the China economic region, consisting of the mainland, Taiwan, Hong Kong, and Macao, will continue to progress.

Economic integration in the China region is widely accepted by international economic institutions and the media. World economic regionalization and integration will also promote integration and development in the China economic region. Only through regional economic integration can Taiwan, Hong Kong, Macao, and the mainland compete in the world economy of the twenty-first century.

After the mainland and Taiwan enter the WTO, Taiwan, Hong Kong, Macao, and the mainland will all be members of that important international economic organization. They can cooperate within the WTO framework while advancing the economic integration of the China region. Hong Kong is already highly open. Macao will develop faster after returning to China. Taiwan and the mainland, sharing the same cultural identity, can open to each other and the world. Current cross-strait political conflicts and division should not be barriers to common cross-strait economic interests.

Hong Kong's economy will not be influenced by the mainland and Taiwan entering the WTO. Hong Kong will continue to play an important role in economic and trade intercourse and economic integration between the two sides. Before China's unification, Hong Kong, under the "one-country, two-systems" policy, will remain a buffer zone, a business springboard for those from Taiwan and abroad investing in China. Those from Taiwan who are successful in mainland business will be likely to list on the Hong Kong stock exchange. Already more than 10 Taiwan-invested enterprises are so listed. Hong Kong is building a "digital harbor" to attract Taiwan's high-tech enterprises. Enterprises from the United States, Japan, and Taiwan have already invested $1.2 billion in factories to produce 8-inch silicon wafers. This may give impetus to Taiwan's semiconductor industry to enter the mainland market through Hong Kong, with Hong Kong becoming a financial center as small- and medium-size enterprises from Taiwan, Hong Kong, Macao, and the mainland raise needed capital.

After the mainland and Taiwan enter the WTO, economic and trade relations within the China economic region will widen.

First, capital flows and capital mergers between the two sides will increase. Capital flows among Taiwan, Hong Kong, Macao, and the mainland are increasing, although it remains difficult for mainland capital to enter Taiwan. Taiwan's banking industry has invested to make Hong Kong a financial base for the China economic region. In addition, Hong Kong is a springboard for Taiwan securities to enter the mainland and Southeast Asian markets.

Second, regional resource allocation will be optimized as a reasonable industrial division of labor comes into the China economic region. This division of labor is not vertical, as some in Taiwan expect, but rather based broadly on the region's resources, technology, human power, geographic location, and economic development level. After the mainland and Taiwan enter the WTO, regional business will naturally see China as Taiwan, Hong Kong, and Macao's economic hinterland, while Hong Kong and Taiwan will be two important frontier windows for China's economic development.

Last, the mainland and Taiwan's entering the WTO will accelerate economic and trade exchange and personnel exchange, shaping a highly developed business corridor within the China economic region. This in turn will facilitate two-way transportation, tourism, and commerce and spur economic prosperity in the whole region. Trade volume among Taiwan, Hong Kong, Macao, and the mainland has already reached $900 billion. This is a solid basis for integrated regional development. If Taiwan opens its tourism to the mainland, Taiwan's tourism industry will accelerate as will tourism throughout the region. Such would further integrate regional economic development.

In conclusion, the entry of mainland China and Taiwan into the WTO holds great economic promise—for the economic growth of the mainland and Taiwan, for the acceleration and opening of cross-strait economic interaction, and for the integration and development of the China economic region.

CHAPTER NINE

TAIWAN'S ECONOMIC INFLUENCE: IMPLICATIONS FOR RESOLVING POLITICAL TENSIONS

Lee-in Chen Chiu

SINCE PRESIDENT LEE TENG-HUI PROPOSED a "special state-to-state relationship" to define political China-Taiwan relations, political tension between the two sides has intensified considerably. Politicians, government officials, military authorities, and scholars have said much on all sides on the issue. Little has been said geared toward peacefully resolving the tension. Including economists in this dialogue is timely.

The sovereignty dispute between China and Taiwan is the result of a half-century of poverty, war, natural and man-made disasters, and invasions. In the new century, world leaders should work for a war- and disaster-free world, emphasizing enhanced public welfare. How Taiwan and China resolve their differences may one day be a model for conflict resolution elsewhere in the world, especially in Asia.

An old Chinese adage says, "The kind become kings." Taiwan has sought respectful and mutually beneficial relations with China and its other neighboring countries for years. From the 1980s, Taiwan entrepreneurs have invested billions of dollars in Southeast Asia and China. Even during the most difficult period of the Asian financial crisis, Taiwan entrepreneurs maintained their regional investments in contrast to Japanese and Korean investors who withdrew billions of dollars worth of capital and bank loans. The evidence suggests that Taiwan-invested industries have become a linchpin of regional economic stability.

Here I explain the importance of Taiwan's maintaining its political neutrality in the Asia-Pacific region so that Taipei can continue to be a stabilizing influence on the regional economy. If the People's Republic of China (PRC) continues to insist that Taiwan is part of China, ensuing tensions will undermine regional economic recovery. Taiwan's economic importance deserves worldwide attention and is worth preserving until Taiwan's people are willing to determine their nationality identity.

I elaborate how the Republic of China (ROC) government formulated its policy on the division of labor across the Taiwan Strait so as to protect Taiwan industry and review in detail Taiwan's recent investment and trade policies. I illustrate how Taiwan's manufacturing capabilities and industrial networks contributed to regional economic stability during the Asian financial crisis. Building on that analysis, I suggest how Taiwan's significant economic status can be used to resolve regional political tensions.

A sound model for China-Taiwan conflict resolution could one day contribute to peace and prosperity for other troubled areas in the world.

ECONOMIC INTERACTION BETWEEN TAIWAN AND CHINA: INVESTMENT POLICIES ON THE DIVISION OF LABOR ACROSS THE TAIWAN STRAIT

After the ROC government withdrew to Taiwan in 1949, owing to political hostility, any trade or business activity with mainland China was regarded as treason. This fact is illustrated by the "Regulations on the Prohibition of Commercial Products from Bandit-Controlled Areas" legislation of 1977. According to this regulation, only a very few herbal medicines and necessary agricultural or industrial materials are allowed to be indirectly imported through Hong Kong. In 1985, the ROC for the first time responded to the demand for trade between the two sides of the Taiwan Strait and announced its "Noninterference Principle of Indirect Exports to Mainland China." Since then, the trade volume between the two sides of the Taiwan Strait has

Table 9.1
Estimation of the Indirect Trade Volume between Taiwan and Mainland China
Unit: U.S.$ millions, rates in percent

Year	Taiwan to Mainland China (A)		Mainland China to Taiwan (B)		Estimation by Mainland Affairs Council (C)			
	Trade Volume	Growth Rate	Trade Volume	Growth Rate	Export Volume	Growth Rate	Import Volume	Growth Rate
1978	0.05	—	46.68	—	—	—	—	—
1979	21.47	42,840.00	56.27	20.54	—	—	—	—
1980	234.97	994.41	76.21	35.44	—	—	—	—
1981	384.15	994.41	75.18	-1.35	—	—	—	—
1982	194.45	-49.38	84.02	11.76	—	—	—	—
1983	157.84	-18.83	89.85	6.94	—	—	—	—
1984	425.45	169.55	127.75	42.18	—	—	—	—
1985	986.83	131.05	115.09	-9.28	—	—	—	—
1986	811.33	-17.78	144.22	24.43	—	—	—	—
1987	1,226.53	51.18	288.94	100.35	—	—	—	—
1988	2,242.22	82.81	478.69	65.67	—	—	—	—
1989	2,896.49	29.18	586.90	22.61	3,331.9	—	586.9	—

Table 9.1 (continued)
Estimation of the Indirect Trade Volume between Taiwan and Mainland China
Unit: U.S.$ millions, rates in percent

Year	Taiwan to Mainland China (A)		Mainland China to Taiwan (B)		Estimation by Mainland Affairs Council (C)					
	Trade Volume	Growth Rate	Trade Volume	Growth Rate	Export Volume	Growth Rate	Import Volume	Growth Rate		
1990	3,278.26	13.18	765.36	30.41	4,394.6	31.89	765.4	30.40		
1991	4,667.15	42.36	1,125.95	47.11	7,493.5	70.52	1,125.9	47.10		
1992	6,287.90	34.77	1,119.00	-0.62	10,547.6	40.75	1,119.0	-0.61		
1993	7,585.40	20.63	1,103.60	-1.38	13,993.1	32.67	1,103.6	-1.38		
1994	8,517.20	12.28	1,292.30	17.10	16,022.5	6.94	1,858.7	68.42		
1995	9,882.80	16.03	1,574.20	21.81	19,433.8	21.29	3,091.4	66.32		
1996	9,717.60	-1.67	1,582.40	0.52	20,727.3	6.66	3,059.8	-1.02		
1997	9,715.10	-0.03	1,746.80	10.20	22,455.2	8.34	3,915.4	27.96		
1998	8,364.10	-0.14	1,654.90	-0.05	19,840.9	-0.12	4,110.5	5.00		

Notes: 1. Data in columns (A) and (B) are according to Hong Kong Customs Statistics. Because the volume usually is underestimated, the Mainland Affairs Council enacted in1989 a new estimation method that takes the Customs Statistics of Taiwan, mainland China, and Hong Kong into consideration. The estimation of the Mainland Affairs Council is in column (C).
2. The growth rates are as compared with the same period of the previous year.

grown steadily (see Table 9.1), except for a period of negative growth in 1996 caused by PRC internal adjustments of foreign trade policy.

Investment from Taiwan to China increased when the ROC government began to soften its hostile political attitude toward the PRC in 1987. In the same year, the ROC announced two important policies affecting mainland China. One nullified martial law. The other granted permission for Taiwan citizens to visit relatives in China. Taiwan entrepreneurs were quick to sense the change in the political atmosphere between Taiwan and China. Although certain cases of family-related investments had been in evidence since 1982, open indirect investments did not emerge until after 1987.

Basically, Taiwan-China economic interaction can be described in two stages: 1978–1986, trade inception, and 1987 to the present, investment inception.

Economic interaction across the strait was legalized on September 18, 1992, when the "Statute Governing Relations between Peoples of the Taiwan Area and the Mainland China Area" came into effect. Following the statute, in 1993, four regulations governing the approval of trade, investment, and technical cooperation; banking exchange; and insurance exchange were promulgated. Under these new economic regulations Taiwan's government planned its industrial network system for the production division of labor across the Taiwan Strait.

The goals of this production division of labor across the Taiwan Strait were to maintain the industrial strength of Taiwan and to control the flow and direction of investment. Collective investment regulations are important for an economy dominated by small- and medium-size enterprises (SMEs), such as Taiwan's.

Two main tools were used to implement the division-of-labor policy: control of the contents of imported goods and control of the contents of invested products and technical cooperation. According to current data, 55.13 percent (or 5,644 items out of 10,238 harmonized system [HS] coded 10-digit trade commodities) are permitted to be imported indirectly from China to Taiwan. Regarding investment control, every six months the Ministry of Economic Affairs reviews approximately 8,000 items of HS coded 8-digit commodities and classifies them into either permitted items, prohibited items, or case-by-case evaluation items. By September 1999, 6,658 items were classified as permitted and only 342 items as prohibited.

The major criterion for permitting items is that they have no negative effect on national security and domestic industries. There are four criteria for prohibited items: COCOM (Coordinating Committee for Multilateral Export Controls) limited products or technology, national defense related products, leading new products, or key components and products.

The ROC government regulates the division of labor between Taiwan and mainland China primarily for the purpose of national economic security. Local foreign direct investment (FDI) firms also have their own agenda on technology transfers to their China-based subsidiaries (Figure 9.1). The government does not interfere in this area. Basically, the industrial policy on the division of labor across the Taiwan Strait is regarded as a necessary measure.

Under clear rules, investment from Taiwan to China grew steadily from 1992 to 1996 (Table 9.2). In 1997 contracted investment volume started to fall dramatically following the PRC missile tests and military exercises in waters close to Taiwan. President Lee responded with a new go-slow (so-called no-hurry, be-patient) policy. The Taiwan Strait's 10-year economic and political honeymoon period (1987–1996) had ended and mainland China was to blame.

Regular cross-strait discussions and exchange activities between SEF (Straits Exchange Foundation) and ARATS (Association for Relations Across the Taiwan Strait), the respective negotiation agencies of Taiwan and China, broke off in 1996. PRC officials continued to claim that Taiwan is just another province of China, not a sovereign state. At the Sino-U.S. summit in June 1998 in Shanghai, President Clinton announced his three no's policy that led to President Lee's "special state-to-state" statement.

The contribution of Taiwan investment in China at a time when China's economy was taking off is widely acknowledged. The industrial networks built by Taiwan businesses benefited FDI firms, as Table 9.3 shows with the industrial composition of Taiwanese and Japanese FDI in Tungguan. (Tungguan was originally a small town in

Figure 9.1
Taiwan's Industrial Policies toward Mainland China:
Production Division of Labor across the Taiwan Strait

Policy Goal:
"The roots remain in Taiwan, the leaves stretch over China"

Policy Tools:
Legalization of economic interaction across the Taiwan Strait:

1 "Statute Governing Relations between the Peoples of the Taiwan Area and the Mainland Area," promulgated September 18, 1992.
2 "Regulations Governing the Approval of Investment or Technical Cooperation in Mainland China," promulgated March 1, 1993.
3 "Regulations Governing the Approval of Trade with Mainland China," promulgated April 26, 1993.

Content:

1. Trade:

- No constraints on exporting to mainland China.
- Import permission system in agricultural (472) and industrial (5,172) products. (Up to September 1999, 55.13% of trade commodities are permitted to be imported indirectly from China to Taiwan, $55.13\% = \frac{5644}{10238}$).

2. Investment:

- National security.
- Must not negatively affect domestic industries.

	Permitted Items		Prohibited Items		Case-by-Case Evaluation Items	
	April '97	Sept. '99	April '97	Sept. '99	April '97	Sept. '99
Agriculture	222	215	9	9	8	15
Manufacturing	4,842	6,658	299	342	2,518	702
Tertiary (medium classif.)	21	30	3	3	50	41

3. Go-slow policy from July 1997; applied to multinational and infrastructure investments only.

Table 9.2
Estimation of Indirect Investment by Taiwan in Mainland China
Unit: U.S.$ millions

Year	Approved by Ministry of Economic Affairs, ROC			Announced by PRC				
	Case	Amount	Average Scale	Case	Contracted Amount	Average Scale	Realized Amount	Realized Ratio (%)
To								
1991	237	174.16	0.73	3,884	3,537	0.91	869	24.41
1992	264	246.99	0.94	6,430	5,543	0.86	1,050	18.94
1993	9,329	3,168.41	0.43	10,948	9,965	0.91	3,139	31.50
1994	934	962.21	1.03	6,247	5,395	0.86	3,391	62.85
1995	490	1,092.71	2.23	4,778	5,777	1.21	3,162	54.73
1996	383	1,229.24	3.21	3,184	5,141	1.61	3,475	67.59
1997*	8,725	4,334.31	0.50	3,014	2,814	0.93	3,289	116.88
1998	1,284	2,034.62	1.58	2,970	2,982	1.00	2,915	97.75
To 1998	21,646	13,242.66	0.61	41,017	40,400	0.98	21,265	52.64

*According to Article 35 in "The Statute Governing Relations between Peoples of the Taiwan Area and the Mainland Area," Taiwanese enterprises that invest in mainland China are allowed to complete or make up registration in three months (July–September 1997). Hence the figures above include those approvals of make-up registrations.

Sources: 1. Taiwan Data from Investment Commission, Ministry of Economic Affairs (MOEA), ROC.

2. Mainland China Data from the Ministry of External Trade and Economic Cooperation, PRC.

3. Data are compiled from *Economic and Trade Statistics Across the Strait Monthly* 69 (1998), Mainland Affairs Council.

Guangdong province. It developed over 10 years into a medium-size city in large part because of Hong Kong and Taiwan investment.) The industrial classifications of the FDI firms of these two countries are very similar. More than one-third of the FDI firms shown invested in electrical and electronics machinery and components. The industrial network of the Taiwan investors spreading to Tungguan attracted the Japanese. A similar process is being repeated in other Chinese cities and provinces of China, for example, Kunshan and Suzhou in Jiangsu and Ningbo and Yuyao in Zhejiang. Foreign FDI firms have learned to use the industrial networks and personal connections established

Table 9.3
Industrial Composition of Taiwanese and Japanese Investment in Tungguan City (1996)
Unit: U.S.$ millions, ratios in %

	Sum	Electronics & Machinery	Chemical	Metals	Fiber & Garment	Food	Pulp & Paper
Taiwanese in Tungguan	1,873	657	108	144	103	14	56
Ratio (%)	(100)	(35.1)	(5.8)	(7.7)	(5.5)	(0.7)	(3.0)
Japanese in Tungguan	777	259	98	54	79	55	5
Ratio (%)	(100)	(33.3)	(12.6)	(6.9)	(10.2)	(7.1)	(0.6)

	Leather	Log & Furniture	Brick	Other Manuf.	Service	Agri-culture	Other
Taiwanese in Tungguan	355	80	54	283	103	7	14
Ratio (%)	(19.0)	(4.3)	(2.9)	(15.1)	(5.5)	(0.4)	(0.7)
Japanese in Tungguan	10	8	20	34	138	14	3
Ratio (%)	(1.3)	(1.0)	(2.6)	(4.4)	(17.8)	(1.8)	(0.4)

Source: Straits Exchange Foundation (SEF), no. 92, August 10, 1999.

by Taiwan and Hong Kong businesses. In the past decade, the major industrial networks built by Taiwan entrepreneurs have switched from textiles, shoemaking, and plastic product industries to electronics, personal computers, telecommunications, and their related components and periphery industries.

During the Asian financial crisis, because the PRC did not depreciate its currency, the renminbi, many Taiwan firms in China encountered difficulties in obtaining export orders. Yet managers of Chinese subsidiaries of Taiwan firms generally managed to maintain basic working conditions for their regular employees. For example, when production lines were idle, Taiwan managers arranged for workers to clean yards or warehouses or paint to maintain employment. Taiwan

SMEs provide an income for hundreds of thousands of families in Chinese cities and in Southeast Asia.

Unfortunately, owing to challenges from PRC economic and political reform, the benefits of Taiwan investment have not spread to other localities in China. According to the Ministry of Economic Affairs (ROC), China investment registration statistics of 1991–1997 and 1998 show that the location and industrial distribution of investment tended to be concentrated in the same areas. Originally, the top five Taiwan-invested areas added up to 86.9 percent among 30 provinces (including autonomous regions and cities) from 1991 to 1997: Guangdong, 32.93 percent; Jiangsu (including Shanghai), 30.94 percent; Fujian, 12.14 percent; Hebei, 6.52 percent; and Zhejiang, 4.37 percent. The newly registered cases in 1998 show a bias toward two provinces: Guangdong, 40.52 percent, and Jiangsu, 34.15 percent. The next three are Fujian, 7.41 percent; Hebei, 4.54 percent; and Zhejiang, 4.22 percent.

The industrial concentration ratio of the top five industries among 18 subindustries is also rising. The accumulated invested industries of the top five were 52.54 percent in 1991–1997. In 1998, this ratio jumped to 61.44 percent.

If China's political and economic reforms prove ineffective, regional discrepancies and rural–urban disparities in China will widen. The ROC government offered assistance in agriculture in 1995 and in state-owned enterprise reform in 1998, but these offers were rejected (Figure 9.2).

TAIWAN'S STABILIZATION DURING THE ASIAN FINANCIAL CRISIS

The stabilization effects of Taiwan's economic influence were even more masked in the case of Southeast Asia during the Asian financial crisis. Taiwan's FDI to Southeast Asia equaled that going to the PRC, although the number of firms investing was fewer. (This means mostly medium- and large-size Taiwan enterprises invested in Southeast Asia.) Taiwan is the second-largest investor in Malaysia and Vietnam; the third-largest in Cambodia and China; and the fourth- to

Figure 9.2
Taipei's Olive Branches

Dates	Events
1. April 30, 1991	**Ending Offensive Strategic Posture.** ROC president Lee Teng-hui proclaims an end to the Period of National Mobilization for Suppression of the Communist Rebellion and pronounces that the ROC government renounces the use of military force for the pursuit of national unification.
2. April 8, 1995	**Proposing Cross-Strait Cooperation.** President Lee responds to Chinese president Jiang Zemin's eight-point proposal for cross-strait policy by enunciating a six-point offer to seek cross-strait cooperation on the bases of equality and mutuality.
3. June 12, 1995	**Offering Agriculture Assistance.** At a press conference on his return from the United States, President Lee indicates that cross-strait agricultural cooperation may be a topic for discussion when leaders from Taipei and Beijing meet. He says, "This is not competition, this is mutual assistance so that Chinese people will all prosper."
4. May 20, 1996	**Voyage of Peace.** In his inaugural speech as the ninth president of the ROC, President Lee states that he is willing to undertake a "voyage of peace to the mainland" and to exchange views with Beijing's top leader on the peace, stability, and prosperity of the Asia-Pacific region.
5. April 19,1997	**Off-shore Transshipment Center.** The Off-shore Trans-shipment Center begins operation, which allows ships with flag of convenience (FOC) sailing between Kaohsiung harbor and the harbors of Xiamen and Fuzhou for cargo transshipment to foreign countries.
6. Feb. 19, 1998	**Offering State-owned Enterprise Reform Assistance.** Mainland Affairs Council chairman King-yuh Chang indicates that Taipei is willing to offer assistance for the reform of state-owned enterprises on the mainland.
7. April 17,1998	**Military Transparency.** Premier Vincent Siew proposes exchanges of information on military exercises with the mainland to establish military confidence-building mechanisms, the proposal of which is to avoid misjudgment that may lead to war and to promote military transparency.
8. April 17, 1998	**Joint Effort on Resolving Asian Financial Crisis.** Premier Siew proposes that Taipei and Beijing cooperate in assisting Southeast Asian countries in resolving the financial crisis and to invite them to develop jointly the resources in the South China Sea.

Figure 9.3
Private Capital Flows* from Japan to Asian Crisis–Hit Countries

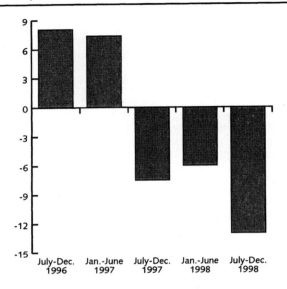

Note: * includes foreign direct investment, portfolio investment, and bank lending.

Source: *Far Eastern Economic Review,* July 29, 1999, p. 53.

sixth-largest in Thailand, Philippines, and Indonesia. As a trade partner, Taiwan ranks between fifth and ninth with each of these countries. Taiwan's geographically wide investment pattern is unusual, especially when Taiwan's per capita income level is considered.

Taiwan's economic stabilization effect in Southeast Asia was tested for the first time by the Asian financial crisis. Although most countries in Southeast Asia were badly hit by the financial crisis, especially during the most difficult period from July 1997 to the end of 1998, Taiwan was able to offer assistance to its neighboring countries. Meanwhile Japan withdrew some U.S.$27 billion of FDI, portfolio investment, and bank lending from the region over one-and-a-half years (Figure 9.3).

Taiwan's industrial networks, which had extended into the region by FDI over the past two decades, also exhibited a strong stabilization effect in maintaining the export competitiveness of host countries.

Table 9.4
Taiwan's Economic Relationship with the PRC and Southeast Asian Countries (to 1998)
Unit: U.S.$ millions

Country	Investment Amount	Number of Cases	Investment Rank in Host Country	Export	Import
PRC	41,017	40,400	3	9	3
Thailand	9,703	1,355	4	5	7
Malaysia	8,582	1,591	2	5	6
Philippines	750	821	5	5	5
Indonesia	13,579	683	6	9	8
Singapore	1,301	295	13 (1995)	6	5
Vietnam	4,737	469	2	6 (1995)	
Cambodia	367	55	3	—	—
SE Asia Total	39,019	5,269	—	—	—

Sources:1. Investment data are from the Board of Investment (BOI), Thailand; Malaysian Industrial Development Authority (MIDA), Malaysia; Board of Investment (BOI), the Philippines; (Badan Koordinasi Penanaman Modal-Investment Coordinating Board BKPN), Indonesia; Economic Development Board (EDB), Singapore; Ministry of Planning and Industry (MPI), Vietnam; Commission on Investment and Business (CIB), Cambodia; and Ministry of Foreign Economic, Trade and Commerce (MFETC), PRC (provided by the Department of Investment, Ministry of Economic Affairs [MOEA], ROC).
2. Trade ranking in Southeast Asian countries from <www.moeaboft.gov.tw/> and <www.sear.cier.edu.tw/>, varied months in 1999.

Taiwan investors poured relatively large amounts of capital into food processing (especially animal or vegetable fats and oils), textiles, and garment and footwear in Indonesia; food and beverage processing and electronic and electrical appliances in Thailand; and electronic and electrical appliances in Malaysia (Table 9.4). These industries showed stable export competitiveness before and after the financial crisis (Table 9.5). In fact, the industrial competitiveness of Southeast Asian countries in the U.S. market was only mildly influenced by the Asian financial crisis (Table 9.6).

Also evidence of Taiwan's economic influence in Southeast Asia is the recovering market share in Japan's market as the worst

Table 9.5
Statistics on Approved Outward Investment by Area and Industry
Unit: U.S.$ thousands

Area Industries	Hong Kong	Singapore	Philippines	Indonesia	Thailand	Malaysia	Vietnam	Others	Asia Total
Food & Beverage Processing	550 (0.48)	51 (0.02)	20,715 (4.13)	11,413 (2.39)	75,832 (9.62) S	404 (0.03)	110,236 (16.41)	4,680 (8.31)	223,881 (5.32)
Textile	16,316 (14.10)	16,660 (7.64)	44,394 (8.85)	70,874 (14.83) S	36,944 (4.69)	184,800 (14.17)	142,765 (21.15)	2,428 (4.31)	528,861 (12.56)
Garment & Footwear	245 (0.21)	7,765 (3.56)	5,868 (1.17)	17,534 (3.67) S	1,711 (0.22)	1,374 (0.11)	20,006 (2.98)	3,500 (6.22)	62,902 (1.49)
Leather & Fur Products	430 (0.37)	288 (0.13)	1,800 (0.36)	—	2,323 (0.29)	—	4,540 (0.68)	—	9,645 (0.23)
Lumber & Bamboo Products	2,144 (1.85)	1,067 (0.49)	—	2,131 (0.45)	7,722 (0.98)	32,091 (2.46)	5,292 (0.79)	28,940 (51.40)	79,499 (1.89)
Paper Products & Printing	9,994 (8.64)	—	2,187 (0.44)	86,539 (18.11)	20,729 (2.63)	344 (0.03)	109,069 (16.23)	—	228,979 (5.44)
Chemicals	9,588 (8.27)	1,259 (0.58)	110,162 (21.96)	30,165 (6.31)	131,461 (16.67)	105,763 (8.11)	40,753 (6.07)	1,100 (1.95)	440,557 (10.47)

Rubber Products	1,063 (0.92)	9,223 (4.23)	569 (0.11)	36,083 (7.55) **S**	29,358 (3.72)	15,150 (1.16)	9,346 (1.39)	510 (0.91)	102,142 (2.43)
Plastic Products	1,331 (1.15)	3,236 (1.48)	2,100 (0.42)	12,489 (2.61)	6,445 (0.82)	1,192 (0.09)	4,650 (0.69)	—	31,443 (0.75)
Non-metallic Minerals	7,824 (6.76)	4,681 (2.15)	139,421 (27.79)	66,900 (14.00)	18,585 (2.36)	34,291 (2.63)	118,189 (17.59)	21 (0.04)	392,590 (9.33)
Basic Metals & Metal Products	1,140 (0.99)	4,870 (2.23)	11,273 (2.25)	36,254 (7.59)	66,612 (8.45)	478,322 (36.68)	14,565 (2.17)	6,563 (11.66)	620,102 (14.73)
Machinery Equipment	6,177 (5.34)	766 (0.35)	600 (0.12)	1,436 (0.30)	5,608 (0.71)	13,449 (1.03)	18,386 (2.74)	183 (0.33)	48,273 (1.15)
Electronic & Electrical Appliances	55,123 (47.63)	168,142 (77.13)	161,681 (32.23)	75,903 (15.88)	384,708 (48.79) **S**	432,784 (33.18) **S**	40,347 (6.00)	6,040 (10.73)	1,357,261 (32.24)
Transport Equipment	13 (0.01)	—	400 (0.08)	29,644 (6.20)	398 (0.05)	2,708 (0.21)	29,993 (4.46)	70 (0.12)	63,226 (1.50)
Precision Instruments	3,810 (3.29)	—	455 (0.09)	526 (0.11)	—	1,535 (0.12)	3,789 (0.56)	2,272 (4.04)	20,055 (0.48)
Total	**115,728** (100.00)	**218,008** (100.00)	**501,625** (100.00)	**477,891** (100.00)	**788,436** (100.00)	**1,304,207** (100.00)	**671,926** (100.00)	**56,307** (100.00)	**4,209,416** (100.00)

Note: Those industries designated S are those that showed the strongest export competitiveness before and after the Asian financial crisis as shown in Table 9.6.
Source: *Statistics on Approved Outward Investment by Area and Industry*, Investment Commission, Ministry of Economic Affairs, 1999.

Table 9.6
Comparison of Changes in the Revealed Comparative Advantages (RCA) Index Before and After the Asian Financial Crisis in the U.S. Market (by Industry)

Industry	PRC bef	aft	ROC bef	aft	Indonesia bef	aft	Thailand bef	aft	Malaysia bef	aft	S. Korea bef	aft
Animal Products	W	W	W	W	R	R	S	S	W	W	W	W
Vegetable Products	W	W	W	W	R	R	R	M	W	W	W	W
Animal and Vegetable Fats & Oils	W	W	W	W	S	S	W	W	S	S	W	W
Prepared Foods	W	W	W	W	R	R	S	S	W	W	W	W
Mineral Products	W	W	W	W	W	W	W	W	W	W	W	W
Chemical Products	W	W	W	W	W	W	W	W	W	W	W	W
Plastics & Rubber	R	R	R	R	S	S	R	R	R	R	M	M
Leather	S	S	M	M	R	S	R	S	W	W	R	M
Wood	W	W	W	W	S	S	W	W	W	W	W	W
Paper Pulp & Paper Articles	W	W	W	W	W	W	W	W	W	W	W	W
Textiles	R	R	R	M	S	S	R	R	W	W	R	R
Foot- and Headgear	S	S	W	W	S	S	R	R	W	W	M	W

Category									
Cement, Glass, Ceramics	R	R	W	W	M	M	M	W	W
Textiles	R	R	R	S	S	R	R	W	R
Foot- and Headgear	S	S	W	W	S	S	R	M	W
Cement, Glass, Ceramics	R	R	W	W	M	M	M	W	W
Precious Stones	W	W	W	R	W	W	R	W	W
Base Metals	W	W	R	R	W	W	W	W	M
Mechanical & Electrical Equipment	M	M	R	R	W	W	R	S	S
Transport Equipment	W	W	R	R	W	W	W	W	W
Precision Instruments	M	M	R	R	**W**	**M**	W	W	W
Arms and Ammunition	W	W	W	W	W	W	W	W	M
Miscellaneous Manufactures	S	S	W	W	R	M	**R**	**M**	R
Art & Antiques	W	W	W	W	W	W	W	W	W
Others	W	W	M	M	W	W	W	W	W

Notes: 1. It is assumed that the period 1966.7–1997.4 is before the financial crisis; the period 1997.7–1998.4 is after the crisis.

2. **S**, industries with the strongest export competitiveness; **R**, industries with strong export competitiveness; **M**, industries with medium export competitiveness; and **W**, industries with weak export competitiveness.

3. Figures in bold indicate industrial change in the RCA.

Source: Yu Jun-min, *Weekly Review of Global Situation* 1253 (1998), pp. 14–15. Data of this research come indirectly from Wang Jian-chuan et al., *Research into How the Asian Financial Turmoil Has Influenced Taiwan Industrial Competitiveness* (June 1999), p. 31.

Table 9.7
Share Rate of the Japanese Import Market (by Country)
Unit: %

	1996	1997	1998	1999 (Jan.–June)
United States	22.72	22.34↓	23.95↑	23.38→
United Kingdom	2.05	2.12↑	2.09↓	1.94↓
Germany	4.06	3.67↓	3.81→	3.84→
France	1.79	1.70↓	2.04↑	2.00→
Italy	1.94	1.75↓	1.82↓	1.63↓
Switzerland	1.02	1.01→	1.07↑	1.12↑
Canada	2.90	2.89↓	2.74↓	2.63↓
South Korea*	4.57	4.30↓	4.30↓	4.88↑
R.O.C.*	4.28	3.69↓	3.65↓	4.23↑
Hong Kong*	0.74	0.66↓	0.62↓	0.60↓
Singapore*	2.10	1.73↓	1.68↓	1.86→
Philippines*	1.30	1.48↑	1.58↑	1.65↑
Malaysia*	3.37	3.36↓	3.09↓	3.44↑
Indonesia*	4.35	4.32↓	3.86↑	3.88↑
Australia	4.08	4.31↑	4.64↑	4.18↓
P.R.C.*	11.58	12.36↑	13.22↑	13.32↑

Note: * countries affected by the Asian financial crisis.

Source: *Economic and Statistical Indicators,* Department of Statistics, Ministry of Economic Affairs, 1999.

effects of the Asian financial crisis wane. As Table 9.7 illustrates, all Taiwan-invested countries (e.g., the PRC, Indonesia, Malaysia, and the Philippines) increased their market share in the Japanese market, whereas Hong Kong and Singapore still lagged in 1999.

Additional behind-the-scenes elements can be elaborated. Taiwan's regional economic influence can be attributed to two important factors. One is the flexible management style of large numbers of outward-investing SMEs. Based on their international trade and production division of labor experience, these SMEs have developed a unique sensitivity to exchange rates and a sophisticated means of distributing export orders among subsidiaries to show profits in stable times or to sustain minimum operations during crises.

The other factor is the Taiwan government's policies on the production division of labor across the Taiwan Strait, its "go south" investment policy, and its commitment to implementing related policy measures.

After the challenge of the Asian financial crisis, Taiwan gained a reputation for being able to cope with unexpected economic turbulence in manufacturing and overseas management capability. The ability of Taiwan entrepreneurs to tally the exchange rate, select production costs, and manage cross-border business reflects four decades of export-oriented policies. Such capabilities should be seen not only as Taiwan's asset but also as that of the regional economy.

CONCLUSION:
ECONOMIC AND POLITICAL STABILITY

Taiwan's contribution to a stable regional economy is evident. Without doubt, FDI is an engine of economic reform and development in China. Taiwan investors are important pioneers, establishing industrial networks for latecomers in the PRC.

Another Chinese adage, "Human dignity is not the offspring of an empty stomach," can also mean, "Civilization begins with promoting people's livelihood." Asia has long suffered under various political, ethnic, and economic conflicts. Drawing on its closely knit industrial networks scattered around the region, Taiwan suggested a joint Taiwan-PRC effort to resolve the Asian financial crisis. But the offer was rejected out of hand.

Creating job opportunities for economically vulnerable groups and providing social services to socially vulnerable groups is the highest responsibility of political leaders. Taiwan's regional industrial network is ready and able to deliver such social services in the Asia-Pacific region. Some nongovernmental organizations (NGOs) and charity associations (e.g., Buddhist Compassion Relief Tzu Chi Foundation and the Dharma Drum Mountain Foundation) are already providing such services domestically and internationally. The major donors of these funds include successful SME entrepreneurs. If Taiwan could be integrated into the United Nation's official international assistance or NGO system, it would benefit those most vulnerable in the region.

The ROC has been an independent sovereign state since its founding in 1912, possessing all the characteristics of an independent state (e.g., a standing army, citizenry, a constitution, and territory). If a "special state-to-state" relationship is not acceptable to the PRC, it would be wise to make suggestions acceptable to both sides, for example, a state-equivalent seat in the United Nations for the ROC, a commonwealth political framework, a Chinese Union of States, or a federal government of states. Such measures would be more constructive than threatening the island with military force. The ultimate hope of Taiwan's people is simply to gain equal representation in the international community.

After 400 years of immigration to this beautiful island, those in Taiwan appreciate their ancestors' making a home here. For peace-loving Taiwan, the voices pursuing an independent country will become weaker as long as the country is respected internationally. The wisdom of Chinese ancestors is that "the kind become kings," and "human dignity is not the offspring of an empty stomach." Taiwan is willing to help solve the PRC's internal problems (e.g., by economic reform, modernization, and a democratic political system). Economic assistance is the priority; the question of unification or independence can be left for future generations.

PART FOUR

CONTINGENCIES AND DILEMMAS

CHAPTER TEN

CROSS-STRAIT RELATIONS AND THE PRISONER'S DILEMMA
Chiou I-jen

OVER THE PAST 50 YEARS, the relationship between Taiwan and China has been fundamentally confrontational. This confrontation reflected Cold War structural conflict. A hot war was avoided only through diplomacy. After the Cold War, international conditions changed, but the cross-strait conflict persisted. Sources of the stalemate in cross-strait relations that reflect aspects of a prisoner's dilemma in game theory are outlined here. In a game such as prisoner's dilemma, although it is not in the interest of either side, distrust and lack of mutual confidence inevitably lead both sides to confrontation.

Cross-strait dilemmas take place on three different levels: military, diplomatic, and economic. An analysis of the preference structure and rational choice considerations of both sides follows, starting with the military.

MILITARY DILEMMA

Both Taiwan and China are caught in a military dilemma that fuels an implicit arms race. From China's perspective, maintaining the ultimate option of using force against Taiwan prevents Taiwan from declaring independence. Beijing perceives Taiwan's leaders, particularly Lee Teng-hui, as determined to lead Taiwan toward permanent separation. The threat of force is the last roadblock in Taiwan's path to independence.

China's constant threat of force prompts Taiwan to strengthen its self-defense capabilities. There is concern in Taiwan that even without a declaration of independence a PRC attack is possible. The 1995–1996 missile tests before Taiwan's presidential election only magnified that fear. Besides, in light of China's disproportional weight, without adequate military and economic might to enhance its bargaining strength, Taiwan would not dare sit at the negotiating table with China. Thus Taiwan not only aims at achieving a formidable defense force, but its political leaders also seek to participate in international security arrangements, such as theater missile defense, to increase Taiwan's self-confidence at the bargaining table. China's rapid military buildup across the strait concerns Taiwan. Fearing an imbalance in military strength, Taiwan will also increase its military spending, perpetuating a cycle of arms competition for mutual deterrence across the strait.

Ironically, to avoid losing in a confrontation, distrust and assumed negative intentions have prompted both sides to pursue a path of conflict in the form of an arms race. The threat of force protects China's claimed "territorial integrity," and the acquisition of advanced defense articles helps boost Taiwan's self-confidence at the bargaining table and in a potential military attack.

Following are the rational choice preferences for both sides in a military dilemma:

China's preferences:

1. Taiwan submits to Chinese sovereignty. (China confronts, Taiwan cooperates.)

2. China threatens to use force, engaging the United States to pressure Taiwan against independence. Taiwan responds by upgrading defense capabilities. Potential for war remains. (Mutual confrontation.)

3. China abandons the use of force, and Taiwan agrees not to declare independence. (Both compromise and cooperate.)

4. Taiwan declares independence and China accepts. (Taiwan confronts, China cooperates.)

Taiwan's preferences:

1. China forfeits the use of force and Taiwan declares independence. (Taiwan confronts, China cooperates.)

2. Taiwan upgrades defense capabilities to counter China's threat
to use force. Arms race continues and potential for war remains.
(Mutual confrontation.)

3. China abandons the use of force, and Taiwan agrees not to declare independence. (Mutual compromise and cooperation.)

4. Taiwan surrenders without the cost of war to China. (Taiwan
cooperates, China confronts.)

Because of distrust, both sides doubt the other's sincerity to cooperate. Unilateral cooperation is ruled out, and thus both sides are left
with the only rational choice of confrontation. This is the typical
prisoner's dilemma, reflecting the military dilemma between confrontation and détente.

DIPLOMATIC DILEMMA

Conventional diplomacy is the conduct of relations between sovereign states. In other words, there is no diplomacy without sovereignty. Yet sovereignty being the sore point between China and
Taiwan, diplomatic confrontation has become another battleground.
Many foreign observers find it difficult to comprehend Taiwan and
China's obsession over relations with Tonga or Papua New Guinea
when it is obvious that neither side of the Taiwan Strait has vital interests in these South Pacific nations. The problem is that official diplomatic ties with countries such as Tonga or Papua New Guinea have
deeper symbolic meaning: In the eyes of Taiwan and China, they argue for Taiwan's existence as a sovereign state.

The sovereignty dispute is complicated and sensitive. From China's
perspective, years of imperialist domination by colonial powers in the
nineteenth century resulted in the country being carved up, leaving a
scar of shame. The bearer of 5,000 years of civilization and the
world's most populated country, China aims to reassert itself as a
major world power. The reversion of Hong Kong to PRC sovereignty

was only one part of the recovery of colonial vestiges. Taiwan's separation is interpreted as a remnant of both Japanese colonialism and U.S. imperialism.

Chinese nationalism reflects fundamentally contradictory emotions. On the one hand, China is immensely insecure and shameful about its past of domination by the West. On the other hand, China is also proud of its history as one of the world's greatest ancient empires. This emotional contradiction is manifested in an outpouring of nationalistic sentiments as well as a desperate urgency to prevent Taiwan from permanent separation, even if the cost is war with the United States or Japan.

Thus China insists on a sovereign claim over Taiwan, blocking all access to diplomatic forums that may offer the slightest indication that Taiwan is a sovereign state. The PRC campaign to isolate Taiwan diplomatically has been fueled by Taiwan's assertions of its separate status. This campaign of isolation has only intensified Taiwan's desperation for inclusion in the community of states.

On Taiwan's side, Taipei's self-deception of representing sovereignty on mainland China during the Cold War was replaced by a new sense of national identity as the island democratized in the late 1980s. In the initial cross-strait contact of 1993, both Taiwan and China chose a "mutual cooperation" stance: They agreed on the "one China" principle but disagreed on its definition.

Since then, Taiwan chose to put aside the disputed definition of "one China" and to focus on other issues in cross-strait talks. It became clear that "functional issues" and a step-by-step approach were not enough, for China insisted on Taiwan's compromise on sovereignty as a prerequisite for talks. Over the years, China continued to promote a "three-part theory" on sovereignty: There is only one China, the PRC represents China, and Taiwan is part of China. Under Chinese pressure, this position has been adopted by the international community, which uses it as an excuse to deny Taiwan access to official recognition and international participation on both governmental and nongovernmental levels.

International acceptance of the PRC's interpretation of "one China" has left Taiwan with no room for alternative definitions, contrary to the more open interpretation of the 1993 Koo–Wang agreement. From Taiwan's side, unilateral cooperation in the form of not disputing sovereignty has led only to more international isolation. This is unacceptable to the Taiwanese people who believe they deserve more. Therefore, in the case of losing out over a "Taiwan cooperates, China confronts" situation, President Lee saw himself with no choice but to respond by describing the cross-strait ties as a "special state-to-state relationship" in a desperate attempt to reset the agenda. In the prisoner's dilemma parlance, Taiwan abandoned the lose-win preference in favor of a lose-lose game by confronting China on its sovereignty claims.

China's preferences in the diplomatic dilemma over sovereignty are as follows:

1. Taiwan submits to China's sovereignty, accepting "one China" as a precondition to talks in the direction of a "one country, two systems" formula and putting an end to wasteful spending in diplomatic battles. (China confronts, Taiwan cooperates.)

2. Neither side accepts the other's sovereignty interpretations. The diplomatic battle continues. Taiwan struggles to gain recognition, and China exerts great energy to isolate Taiwan. (Mutual confrontation.)

3. Taiwan reverts to acceptance of the nominal "one China" with a different interpretation—the 1993 Koo–Wang agreement. China allows Taiwan more international space. (Mutual cooperation.)

4. "One China" is no longer a precondition to talks. Both sides deal with each other on an equal basis and the international community recognizes the current separation. Taiwan gains access to international governmental organizations. (Taiwan confronts, China compromises.)

Taiwan's rational choice preference order is as follows:

1. Taiwan and China deal with each other on a special state-to-state relationship. China accepts the reality of Taiwan's separate existence, and both sides engage in talks on an equal basis on issues of

mutual concern. China allows more international activity space for Taiwan. (Taiwan confronts, China cooperates.)

2. There is a suspension of cross-strait dialogue. (Mutual confrontation.)

3. Taiwan reverts to a nominal "one China, different interpretations" condition for talks. The sovereignty dispute is put aside and both sides discuss other issues (functional issues) of mutual concern. (Détente.)

4. Taiwan submits to China's "one country, two systems" formula and forfeits further diplomatic efforts or attempts to gain recognition for Taiwan's sovereignty. (China confronts, Taiwan cooperates.)

China's preference in cross-strait dialogue is naturally a full and legitimate claim to sovereignty and Taiwan's submission. When Beijing interacts with Taiwan, the more it insists on "one China" as a precondition, the stronger will be Taiwan's resistance to talks. But here is the dilemma: China fears that, if it does not insist on its "one China" preference strongly enough by isolating Taiwan internationally, Taiwan's separate sovereignty will gain legitimacy. Taiwan is equally suspicious: Any talk of "one China" could end Taiwan's international existence. Therefore, as long as China sets the agenda for talks based on "one China," Taiwan will choose a noncooperative path. President Lee's two-state theory is a perfect example. With a complete lack of mutual confidence, both sides will continue to take suspiciously cautious strides when interacting with the other, preferring to suspend talks rather than give in to the other's agenda.

ECONOMIC DILEMMA

Many observers, especially those promoting a globalist perspective, argue that close economic engagement is the greatest positive sum, mutual interest area in cross-strait relations. Indeed, business relations have built bridges of mutual interest across the strait and serve as a strong incentive against confrontation. A dilemma also exists in the cross-strait economic relationship: Even as mutual economic interests are found, competitive and even confrontational economic interests are also generated.

The early stages of cross-strait interaction took place in the 1980s in the midst of China's opening and economic reform. The capital market in China was far from mature at the time, and Taiwan business investment in China not only brought in desperately needed foreign capital but also provided Taiwan with an opportunity to upgrade industrially. The labor-intensive, export-oriented manufacturing on which Taiwan relied throughout the 1960s and 1970s faced a bottleneck as Taiwan's labor costs started to rise. Furthermore Taiwan's export quotas were reaching saturation, and Taiwanese businesses gleefully exploited the export quota allotted to Chinese-made products through Taiwan-run companies in China. Gradually, MIT (made in Taiwan) toys and shoes became "made in China," and MIT labels shifted to semiconductors and computers.

The low-skill manufacturing that Taiwanese companies initiated was swiftly adopted by Chinese companies, and these Chinese domestic companies became the chief competitors of Taiwan-owned companies for the Chinese export quota. The PRC government, to protect Chinese companies, established new barriers so that Taiwan lost its comparative advantage over other foreign multinationals.

As mutually complementary manufacturing was replaced by mutual competition, the capital market faced a similar problem. As China developed its own socialist-flavored market economy, and more capital flowed out of Taiwan, China became Taiwan's chief competitor for capital. This competition was apparent during the Asian economic crisis when both sides adopted strategies of domestic spending as a means for recovery. The dramatic increase in domestic capital need revealed the competitive nature of cross-strait capital. The capital shortage for the Taiwan High Speed Rail is an example of how such competition has negatively affected Taiwan's economy.

Besides, increasing and speeding up economic interaction between Taiwan and China have other side effects. Economic growth on both sides will also contribute to the ability of either side to procure or develop more advanced weapons. Thus the potential confrontation across the strait will continue.

Furthermore increasing interaction between both sides in the past decade has spurred development of separate identities. Contact has revealed historical and cultural schisms between the two sides. Polls by various survey centers in Taiwan consistently portray the changing notions of identity in Taiwan. Even as cross-strait business and travel increase, more and more people are identifying themselves as Taiwanese, not Chinese.

Given the above, direct links (or the so-called three links) with China contain a clear dilemma. On the positive side, direct links expand business opportunities and both sides earn the benefits of profits and growth. But, when the cost of business interaction is lowered through direct links, the cost of maintaining national security rises because of heightened mutual suspicion. Furthermore, direct links and increased economic interaction also increase the number of issues to be worked out between the two sides. On the economic side, there are matters such as capital and information flow and means of dispute arbitration to negotiate. On the other side, there are issues related to complicated sovereignty and identity problems, such as tariffs and national flags attached to transportation lines. Political and military dilemmas prevent both sides from negotiating on these purely economic matters. Ultimately, the economic dilemma also results in stalemate.

OVERCOMING THE DILEMMAS

Given the current preference structure of cross-strait interaction, three sets of dilemmas, in military, diplomatic, and economic arenas, all lead to the same result: confrontation. Although confrontation does not necessarily mean military conflict, the possibility exists. From the outside, it is easy to imagine the benefits of mutual cooperation. Both sides can also appreciate those benefits, whether in the form of trade profits, military confidence building to reduce the arms race, or saving dollars through a truce on the diplomatic battlefield. From the inside, on both sides of the strait, internal insecurities, suspicions, and emotional contradictions prevent both sides from reaching the trust needed for mutual compromise.

These cross-strait dilemmas are structural. Assuming that both sides act rationally, there is no internal solution to the preference structure of the prisoner's dilemma. Also, expectations are problematic that the results of Taiwan's presidential election will somehow change the preference order on Taiwan's side, for any rational national leader of Taiwan must consider popular public sentiments. These sentiments become rational as soon as the legitimacy of political leadership depends on them. They are molded by decades of historical differences and will not change in the immediate future. Beyond popular emotions, practical interests also come into conflict, in military, diplomatic, and economic dilemmas.

Since the cross-strait dilemma is structural, avoiding confrontation requires either negotiations in which both sides compromise or outside intervention. The negotiation option is nearly impossible on an official level, because basically even with a negotiated agreement there is no guarantee that both sides will comply; the prisoner's dilemma of mutual suspicion perpetuates this difficulty. For example, Taiwan thinks that agreements in the historic 1993 Koo–Wang talks were not respected.

The other option for changing the preference structure of the dilemma is external intervention, to change the priority order of the rational choices of both sides. The only party capable of playing any intervening role is the United States.

The current policy of the United States is not to mediate or intervene in cross-strait relations. As long as Taiwan and China are unable to break the current stalemate, and as long as the stalemate could result in potential war, U.S. strategic interests in the region may ultimately require the United States to take a more active role in cross-strait relations. Sending envoys to China and Taiwan, following President Lee's description of the state-to-state relationship, as well as high-profile "second track" diplomacy efforts, indicates increasing activity on the part of the United States to prevent a cross-strait conflict. Such activity will continue, whether or not Taiwan and China like it, and such activity will be heightened as long as influencing the rational choices of both sides is deemed necessary to change the current preference structure from conflict to détente.

Some U.S. scholars have presented proposals on interim agreements, specifying a set period of time in which China renounces the use of force and Taiwan forfeits the declaration of independence. In other words, these proposals aim to prolong the status quo until a time when changes on both sides enable mutual compromise. Because of the prisoner's dilemma, agreement is unlikely without an external guarantor.

To begin, both sides will resist agreement for it means significant compromise. Taiwan fears being swallowed up and ceasing to exist internationally, and China fears giving Taiwan an open ticket toward formal separation. Any interim structural agreement must alleviate these fears to be effective. In other words, the interim agreement proposals create new frameworks and opportunities, but there is no guarantee that either side will follow the rules.

Acknowledging that in the near future both sides will adamantly oppose a U.S.-brokered political agreement on "no force, no independence," here I propose that the United States gradually take the guarantor role without specifying the terms on paper. More specifically, the United States must continue defense cooperation with Taiwan and even elevate the level of military contacts and cooperation. Taiwan's increased reliance on the United States for security needs could offer the United States more leverage over Taiwan's decisions in cross-strait relations. Naturally, Taiwan would have more incentive to cooperate with the United States on U.S. interests in China. A better U.S.-Taiwan security relationship would also help to alleviate Taiwan's fears of being swallowed up, while at the same time making the use of force an even more costly option for China.

Beyond strategic power incentives, the United States may gain an opportunity to promote liberal democracy and human rights now. With the collapse of the USSR, the United States became the sole global superpower, making Washington less concerned with the balance of world power but giving it more moral responsibility, as it has shown in Kosovo.

On the economic side, to resolve the dilemma, international intervention is equally important. The best way to govern the cross-strait economic relationship is through international norms and regulations based on market functions, not politically motivated blockades. Only with both sides joining international trade organizations such as the World Trade Organization will their economic and trade interests be regulated by market norms and will Taiwan's insecurities find comfort by joint international efforts at enforcement. The normalization and internationalization of cross-strait trade based on market principles would also help Taiwan gain the confidence to lift the current political- and security-motivated barriers to normal trade.

In conclusion, there is genuine interest in lowering tension and avoiding confrontation. But suspicions overwhelm incentives for cooperation. Outside intervention in changing the preference structure of the prisoner's dilemma provides both cookies and poison: The poison will be accepted only if the cookies are large enough to dilute its effects. The United States is in a difficult position, but global interests also bring global responsibilities.

CHAPTER ELEVEN

LOOKING AHEAD: MAJOR EVENTS THAT MAY AFFECT CROSS-STRAIT RELATIONS

Nancy Bernkopf Tucker

THE CONFRONTATION OF THE UNITED STATES, CHINA, AND TAIWAN during the first decades of a new millennium has dramatic potential: to reach a short- or long-term modus vivendi or to provoke chaos in northeast Asia. Overall, agreement appears to be far less a possibility than disarray and crisis. This is true both because of the fundamental nature of the disputes and because the leaders attempting to confront these problems will not necessarily behave as rational actors when faced with rapidly moving and highly emotional events.

Although the costs of war in the Taiwan Strait clearly and indisputably should be prohibitive for both China and Taiwan, there is nonetheless reason to believe that war could develop there at any time. Coping with such a dangerous reality will not be simple. The challenges arise in several arenas, including military affairs, domestic politics, economic change, and regional disorder.

MILITARY AFFAIRS

There are several events of a military nature that could dramatically alter the security environment across the strait.

PRC Military Action

Since Lee Teng-hui's dramatic July 9, 1999, announcement of his state-to-state formula, Beijing has threatened military action against

Taiwan to demonstrate the unacceptability of Lee's splittist rhetoric and policies. China's leaders have publicly suggested that military reprisal is a virtual certainty with only the venue and timing to be determined. Furthermore, Chinese commentary has suggested that Lee's initiative was more blatantly provocative than his acquisition of a visa to visit the United States in 1995 and that, therefore, China's response must be harsher. Among the most frequently mentioned targets of opportunity are seizure of a small island off China's coast or possibly Itu Aba of the Spratly Islands in the South China Sea.

The fact that no military reprisal has been taken to date does not mean that Beijing has renounced the use of force. Depending on the position adopted by Taiwan's new president after his inauguration in May 2000, Beijing might still turn to its military to administer a cautionary strike or seek retribution.

Any military operation could have a serious impact on the situation in the strait: (1) by leading to war if China miscalculates or Taiwan decides to retaliate in a meaningful way; (2) by prompting U.S. intervention; or (3) by convincing Taiwan finally to abandon the offshore islands to enhance its security. This would sever the "land bridge" between Taiwan and the mainland that Mao Zedong and Chiang Kai-shek wanted to preserve to prevent the emergence of two Chinas.

Chinese military action that was prolonged or involved a blockade would have significant costs for domestic development in China and Taiwan as well as for the United States and the international community. China's belligerence would probably drive away U.S. and European investors in China as well as Taiwan businesses. Moreover, as Taiwan's September 1999 earthquake illustrated, Taiwan's links to the world economy have become so intricate that damage to industry on the island would have global impact; for example, Taiwan's inability to supply computer chips could seriously undermine the capability of giant computer companies abroad to fill orders.

Moreover, the use of military force cannot always be reliably calibrated, and there is considerable risk of an accident producing escalation. Already, there have been incidents of aircraft crossing the mid-strait dividing line between China and Taiwan. Without an effective "hot line" between Taipei and Beijing, which could minimize error and explain unintended provocation, disaster could follow.

Theater Missile Defense

Even without military action by China, the threat and counterthreat of Chinese missiles and Taiwan theater missile defense (TMD) can radically alter the regional security environment. Beijing has refused to acknowledge linkage between TMD and its placement of ballistic missiles on its southern coast, declaring that these deployments are an internal matter. But Taipei sees these missiles as a direct challenge to its security, and, because of the proximity of the island to China, there are few options that will diminish the peril.

Taiwan's security need has triggered a response from the U.S. Congress, many of whose members seem determined to provide TMD to Taiwan regardless of China's heated opposition. In Taiwan, although the actual military value of TMD is debated and the enthusiasm of Taiwan military officials has been slow in coming, there is clear political advantage in showing interest in the system. Lee Teng-hui, at least, understands TMD as a way to reestablish close military cooperation with the United States, which ended with abrogation of the Mutual Defense Treaty in 1980, and perhaps to acquire the technology to make Taiwan an early-warning, forward picket for U.S. forces. The advantages of TMD may come more from working closely with the United States than from the system itself given that TMD remains experimental, cannot intercept cruise missiles, and may provide only a limited shield against missiles traveling the short distance between China and Taiwan.

PRC Military Modernization

China's push to modernize its military forces is apparent and potentially destabilizing. It could spark a regional arms race. In fact, until the Asian economic crisis, the nations of Southeast Asia had already escalated arms purchases. This is even more true of Taiwan, where, for example, Taipei acquired F-16 and Mirage aircraft in response to China's purchase of advanced Su-27 aircraft from Russia. As China develops asymmetrical forces pinpointing U.S. military weaknesses, it will increase Sino-U.S. tensions. Furthermore, as Beijing's urgency regarding Taiwan unification increases, China may finally invest sufficiently in the amphibious capabilities it has always lacked and the Taiwan Strait air superiority vital to a successful conquest of Taiwan. China's decision to accelerate military modernization in these ways would obviously alter the security environment across the strait.

ECONOMIC CHANGE: CRISIS AND WTO ENTRY

Should China fail to cope with its bankrupt state-owned enterprises, insolvent banking system, overbuilt property market, and growing masses of unemployed workers, economic conditions in the region could worsen dramatically. An economically impoverished China would threaten its neighbors and the United States with masses of refugees. Domestic economic collapse would make outside investment difficult and undesirable. Even Taiwan businesses, which have generally been the most determined to stay in the China market, would be forced to move their money elsewhere.

Were investments from Taiwan to slow or stop, the economic ties that Beijing's leaders believe bind Taiwan and the mainland would begin to dissolve. This would eliminate a crucial buffer that keeps China from taking more hostile action against Taiwan because China would then have less to lose. Furthermore, a Chinese leadership confronting economic collapse might be tempted to deflect popular anger by directing a nationalistic campaign against Taiwan. The manipulation of demonstrations following the U.S. bombing of the PRC's Belgrade embassy shows that Chinese leaders might embrace such tactics.

Economic strains are also likely as China and Taiwan enter the World Trade Organization (WTO) and are required to abide by new international trading rules. The barriers that Taiwan has erected to limit Chinese investment on the island may not comply with WTO rules. Taipei will be under renewed pressure to open the three links. As Wang Jianmin elaborates in chapter 8 of this volume, there will have to be major readjustments in these and other areas.

DOMESTIC POLITICS

Elections in Taiwan and the United States in 2000, along with the anticipated retirement of Jiang Zemin in 2002 or 2003, will almost certainly have an impact on cross-strait relations.

Taiwan's Election

Taiwan's March 2000 election has the potential to alter conditions in the area both as a result of the actual balloting and as the campaign develops. It is clear that Lee Teng-hui's state-to-state formula grew out of concern about China's efforts to isolate Taiwan diplomatically and anger at the United States for seeming to tilt toward Beijing. Both Clinton's declaration of the three no's in Shanghai in July 1998 and the subsequent administration advocacy of interim agreements between Taipei and Beijing appeared to jeopardize Taipei's position in cross-strait dialogue. Lee wanted to internationalize the Taiwan issue again. But Lee also appears to have had a domestic political agenda. He sought to serve Kuomintang (KMT) interests and those of his vice president and presumed KMT presidential candidate, Lien Chan, as they grappled with what was shaping up to be a difficult campaign. Lee also wants firmly to establish his own political legacy by committing any successor to his policies. As the election campaign continues, more politically motivated surprises could arise.

Potentially, Taiwan's election could also change party control of government on the island. The Democratic Progressive Party (DPP) probably cannot win, but if Lien Chan and James Soong split KMT votes, a DPP victory is not impossible, something Beijing might see as provocative. Beijing could even find a win by Lien Chan unpalatable if Lien seems obviously dominated by Lee Teng-hui. A new Taiwan president, whomever he might be, if he is not more accommodating than Lee, will make better relations with Beijing difficult to establish.

The U.S. Election

The U.S. presidential election could be a destabilizing factor if Republican contenders use China policy to attack the Clinton administration and Democratic Party. Although George W. Bush is not a foreign policy "wonk" and his ties to the business community and his father tend to moderate any anti-China proclivities, there are concrete gains to be made by playing a China card. Bush and other Republicans can fault the Clinton administration for weakness and vacillation on China policy, especially with regard to human rights, nuclear security, Chinese espionage, campaign finance irregularities, and ineffective controls on satellite technology. Most recently, Republicans have called on the administration to take a strong stand on behalf of defending Taiwan against Chinese attack. As China becomes a campaign issue, friction in the Sino-U.S. relationship will be aggravated, and potential solutions to problems will be delayed or blocked entirely. Whether a new Republican administration would be significantly more pro-Taiwan and anti-China is difficult to predict. Few would have imagined that Bill Clinton would be seen as soft on China when he was campaigning in 1992.

Jiang Zemin's Political Future

Given that Jiang's current term of office ends in 2002, he will likely become more concerned about his legacy. His emphasis on and personal involvement in handling the Taiwan issue create pressure on him to push for some resolution in the near future to complement his success in recovering Hong Kong and Macao.

Another factor that could have a dramatic impact on cross-strait relations would be a significant change in China's approach to the United States. Chinese analysts and policymakers have been reexamining Chinese foreign policy and Sino-U.S. relations for many months. Some Chinese believe Washington has thwarted the PRC at every turn. So far, anger toward the United States has not redirected policy significantly because China continues to need the benefits that only a relationship with the United States can yield: markets and technology. Should either Beijing's calculations or its tolerance for frustration change, however, tension across the strait could worsen precipitously.

REGIONAL DISORDER

Were the cooperative and moderate approaches that Beijing has taken on issues such as the status of and relations between the two Koreas and the retrocession of Hong Kong to change, peace in the region would be endangered.

Korea

Among the most potentially destabilizing developments in the region would be the collapse of North Korea and reunification of the Korean peninsula. Until now, the United States and China have cooperated on Korean affairs. They have largely agreed on giving North Korea humanitarian assistance and settling disputes through negotiation. Should Korea be unified, the picture would change. China does not want unification in the near future because Beijing does not want a strong Korea on the peninsula. Most important, Beijing does not want to confront across its border a unified Korea allied with the United States and hosting U.S. troops. Korean unification could thus become a source of trouble between Washington and Beijing. Alternatively, if, owing to Korean unification, U.S. troops are reduced or deployed only in southern Korea, this could fuel Japanese demands for U.S. troop withdrawals. Either or both of these developments could jeopardize Taiwan's security and increase its sense of vulnerability.

Hong Kong

Serious flaws in the implementation of Beijing's one-country, two-systems model in Hong Kong would inevitably discourage Taiwan from considering reunification seriously. Although Taiwan has already explicitly rejected the PRC's one-country, two-systems formula, the preservation and protection of Hong Kong's autonomy would probably still have a positive effect in Taiwan. But as Hong Kong's autonomy is eroded by disputes over problems such as legal jurisdiction and residency rights, the effect in Taiwan may become increasingly negative.

CROSS-STRAIT DIALOGUE

The analysis here has been largely negative, emphasizing possible disruptive elements that could dramatically alter for the worse the cross-strait political, economic, or security environment. But there is also a chance for better cross-strait relations in the future. Cross-strait talks could stop being used as an arena in which to score political advantage or a battleground on which one side must sacrifice its vision of the future to mollify the other. It is possible to imagine a genuine desire for progress motivating both sides to be creative about providing incentives for compromise. At present, China—the greater power—must accept greater responsibility for innovation since it is Beijing that wants to alter the status quo and bring about reunification.

As for the United States, the future will be volatile and Washington must be prudent. There is little to gain and much to lose if the United States allows Beijing and Taipei to fight their battles in Washington. The United States must not be tempted to mediate an agreement or impose a solution on Taiwan. Washington spent decades promoting democracy on the island. Now that it exists, the United States must deal with it rather than seek to push Taiwan's leaders into a settlement they do not want and cannot defend to Taiwan's electorate. Valuing both self-determination and sovereignty, the United States should not try to choose between them. Similarly, the United States should neither demonize China nor stigmatize Taiwan as a troublemaker. The future would be far more comfortable for the United States if it reduced its involvement in the cross-strait confrontation. It is unlikely, however, that either side will allow this to happen. The only alternative for the United States is to continue to emphasize that any solution to the current impasse must be acceptable on both sides of the strait and must not disrupt regional peace and stability.

INDEX

American Institute in Taiwan (AIT), 88
Asian Development Bank (ADB): bureaucratic inertia in Taiwan, 107–8; Taiwan as member of, 15, 38
Asia-Pacific Economic Cooperation (APEC): Taiwan as member of, 15, 38–9, 60
Association for Relations Across the Taiwan Strait (ARATS), vii, 11, 41, 65, 132
Association of Euro-Asian Studies, Taiwan, 73
Brzezinski, Zbigniew, 24
Bush, Richard, 23
Campbell, Kurt, 25
capital flows, Taiwan, Hong Kong, Macao and China, 125
Chang Jung-feng, 107
Chen Po-chih, 107
Chen Shui-bian, 22, 42, 78
Chiang, P. K., 89
Chao, Chien-min, 70
China: creating instability in Taiwan, 114; current economic problems, 34–5; economic policy to reduce excess capacity, 105–6; in international quality ladder, 98–9; issues of conern related to Taiwan, 8–10; in Lee's seven-lump theory, 21; position on Taiwan's international participation, 58–64; as potential WTO member, 117–9, 121; public opinion in cross-strait relations, 73–4; seat in United Nations, 81; strength in reunification, 26; Taiwan as part of, 68; Taiwanese industry in, 104, 111; Taiwan's investment in, 102, 122–3, 131; Taiwan's sovereignty belongs to, 66; threats of military action against Taiwan, 160–2 See also industrial sector, China; People's Republic of China (PRC); reunification, China-Taiwan

China Credit Information Service (CCIS) survey (August 1999), 45–6, 49–57
China economic region: China, Taiwan, Hong Kong, and Macao, 124–5; factors influencing trade relations in, 125; Hong Kong as financial base for, 125; predicted division of labor, 125
China-Taiwan relations: diplomatic dilemma, 151–4, 156–9; economic, 131–7; economic dilemma, 154–9; interim arrangements, 3-17; Lee's role in, 20–3; military confidence-building measures, 16–7; military dilemma, 149–51, 156–9; potential for cross-strait dialogue, 167; proposals to improve, 27–30; proposal for interim relations, 8–17; proposed development of cross-strait dialogue, 10–3; proposed expansion of cross-strait economic and cultural ties, 13–4; proposed set of mutual reassurances, 8–10
Chung Chin, 102–4, 109–10
Clinton, Bill: on East Timor conflict, 47; remarks about two-state theory, 23; three no's policy, 22, 25, 76, 132; on U.S. one-China policy, 23, 76–7
Clinton administration: actions in framework of China-Taiwan policy, x; outcomes of China policy, 76; position on two-state theory, 23
competition: among Chinese industrial enterprises, 98–9; from China-based MNCs, 114; by China to oppose Taiwan's international space, 67–70
Crawford, James, 85

democracy: Taiwan as, 33; Taiwan's use of idea of, 71–3

Democratic Progressive Party (DPP), Taiwan, 42

Deng Xiaoping, 34, 67–8

economic integration and interaction: in China economic region, 124; cross-strait, xiv, 124, 131

Ernst, Dieter, 109

foreign direct investment (FDI): problems of investment in China, 106; in Taiwan, 102–4; of Taiwan during Asian financial crisis, 136–45; of Taiwan in China, 102, 104, 106–8; of Taiwan toward ASEAN countries, 103

foreign policy, U.S.: China-Taiwan policy framework, ix–x; dual policy toward Taiwan, 24; one-China policy, ix–x, 42; principles as issues in Taiwan Strait, xvi–xvii; proposals related to China-Taiwan relations, 27–30; purpose of policy toward Taiwan, 26; toward Taiwan and china, 76 See also Taiwan Relations Act (1979); Taiwan Security Enhancement Act, proposed

Gilman, Benjamin, 24

Grossman, Gene, 97–8

Helms, Jesse, 24

Helpman, Elhanan, 97–8

Heritage Foundation, 24

Hong Kong: as buffer zone, 125; continued role in trade and economic integration, 124–5; question of future autonomy of, 166; Taiwan's conception of, 36; Taiwan's economic relationship with, 99–100

Hutchison, Kay Bailey, 29

independence: of states in international law, 85; Taiwan's external, 87–8

industrial sector, China: facilities of foreign electronics manufacturers, 111; problems in, 105; reform and evolution of, 98–9; Taiwan investment in and policies for, 131–7

industrial sector, Taiwan: challenges to PC industry, 10–1; electronics industry, 103–4; manufacturing technologies, 100; prediction of electronics industry performance, 109–11; production division of labor, 131–4

interim arrangements: concept of, 3–6; design for proposed, 8–17; validity and desirability of, 6–8

international community: effect of acceptance of Taiwan's sovereignty, 70; nonrecognition of Taiwan by many countries, 80–1; principles related to Taiwan, 68; proposed expansion of Taiwan's role in, 14–5; Taiwan's membership in international organizations, 38–9

international law: criteria for state as a juristic person in, 81–2; of recognition, 80; rights and immunities of states in, 85; sovereignty in theory of, 82–4; Taiwan's status in, 80

international space: defined, xii; Taiwan's, 69–71; Taiwan's seeking, 70–1

investment: by Taiwan in Southeast Asian countries, 136–45; Taiwan's control of flow and direction of, 131–2; from Taiwan to China (1992-1996), 132–6 See also foreign direct investment (FDI)

Jiang Zemin: at APEC summit (1999), 46; eight points under one-China principle, 70; meeting with Yeltsin (198), 34; political future of, 165; visit to United States (1997), 5

Kissinger, Henry, 24

Koo Chen-fu: meeting with Wang (1993), vii; visit to Chinese mainland (1998), vii, 12, 20, 22

Korea: regional destabilizing effect, 166

Krugman, Paul, 97

Kuomintang (KMT) party: Lee as chairman, 41; political liberalization, 86–7

Law for Protection of Investment by Compatriots from Taiwan, China, 35

Law of the Sea, Exclusive Economic Zone: sovereign rights under, 85; of Taiwan, 88

Lee, K. Y., 107

Lee Teng-hui, 4, 5; creating crises (1995, 1999), 63–4; perception of PRC, 75; role in cross-strait relations policy, 77–8; seven-lump theory, 21; strategy for Taiwan's independence, 66–7, 89–90; two-state theory, 5, 8, 12, 14–5, 21, 23–4, 27, 35, 40–3, 59, 63–4, 74–5, 78, 89,

statehood, 82; current role in WTO, 118–9, 123; economic relationship with China, 99–108; elections (March 2000), 22, 27, 77–8, 164, ; entry to WTO, 118–20; external sovereignty, 87–8; FDI in China, 102; in future status quo arrangement, 63–4; ideological disputes with China, 71–3; independence in, 27; industrial sector, 100; internationally recognized principles about, 68; in international quality ladder, 99; investment in China, xiv, 102, 122–3; issues of concern related to China, 8–10; legal status in context of democratic sovereignty, 86–8; one nation, two states policy, 90–1; outflow of capital, technology and workforce, 107; overseas Chinese in, 103; perception of interim arrangements concept, 5–6; position on PRC one-China policy, 36–7, 90–1; potential for political instability, 114; in potential one-China framework, 62; PRC's boycott of, 36; public opinion in cross-strait relations, 73–4; refusal to negotiate with PRC, 70–1; relations with countries of the world, 81–2; seeking international space, 70–1; as sole legitimate representative of China, 66; stabilizing effect during Asian financial crisis, 136–45; status in international law, 80; two-state theory, 68 See also China economic region; China-Taiwan relations; foreign policy, U.S.; investment; Republic of China (ROC); reunification, China-Taiwan; sovereignty; trade; United Nations

Taiwan Independence Party, 43

Taiwan Relations Act (1979): ambiguity and defects of, 25–6; as U.S. foreign policy, ix–x, 4–5, 18, 24–5, 37, 112

Taiwan Security Enhancement Act, proposed, 22, 27, 75

Taiwan Strait: concept of interim arrangements applied to, 3–6; crisis (1995-1996), x, 4, 5; cross-strait relations, 6–8; possibility of arms race, 7–8; production division of labor across, 131–2; U.S. policy related to, 17–8

Tang Jiaxuan, 46

theater missile defense (TMD), 29, 162

Torricelli, Robert, 24

Track Two dialogue: ARATS-SEF, 11

trade: within China economic region, 125; China's potential export volume to Taiwan, 121; cross-strait, 120–4; improved Taiwan-China relations (1992), 131; Taiwan's exports to and imports from Hong Kong and China, 101, 121; volume between China and Taiwan (1978-1998), 128–30

two-state theory (liang guo lun): China's conception of, 14–5; independence of Taiwan based on ideology, 72; of Lee, 5, 21; Lee's timing of announcement, 21–3; Taiwan's equal status with China, 67–8

United Nations: China's seat in, 81; sovereign nations with more than one vote, 37; Taiwan expelled from (1971), 36; Taiwan's effort to rejoin, 37–8

United States: dilemma related to Taiwan, 26–7; dual policy toward Taiwan, 24–7; effect of cross-strait stalemate on role of, 76–7; election (2000), 164–5; one-China policy, 6, 22–3, 26, 42, 112; policy toward Taiwan Strait, 17–8; proposed Taiwan Security Enhancement Act, 27, 75; role in China-Taiwan interim arrangements, 17–8; theater missile defense policy, 29; three no's policy, x, 5, 22; three pillars of China policy, 23 See also foreign policy, U.S.; Taiwan Relations Act (1979); Taiwan Security Enhancement Act, proposed

Vernon, Raymond, 97

Wallance, Rebecca, 84

Wang Daohan, 13; meeting with Koo (1993), vii; postponed visit to Taiwan (1999), vii, 41, 42, 65, 78; vist to Taiwan (2000), 47

weapons: U.S. sales to Taiwan, 24–5, 29, 76

World Trade Organization (WTO): China's potential membership, 106, 117–9; China's preferential treatment under, 121; effect of China and Taiwan entering, 120–6; Taiwan, Penghu, Jinmen, and Matsu Tariff Region, 118–9, 123; Taiwan as observer, 15, 38–9, 60

ABOUT THE CONTRIBUTORS

Richard C. Bush is the chairman of the board and managing director of the American Institute in Taiwan (AIT). Bush was appointed to the AIT board by Secretary of State Madeleine Albright in September 1997. He worked for 12 years on the Democratic staff of the House International Relations Committee, first on the Asian Affairs Subcommittee and later the full committee. Prior to becoming AIT chairman, he served as national intelligence officer for East Asia. Bush holds a Ph.D. in political science from Columbia University.

Lee-in Chen Chiu is a research fellow at Chung-Hua Institute for Economic Research (CIER) as well as an associate professor at the Institute of Town and Planning at Taiwan University. She earned a Ph.D. in regional economics from the University of Pennsylvania. Chen Chiu has published widely on the Chinese economy and cross-strait economic relations.

Chiou I-jen earned his M.A. at the University of Chicago in political science in 1980 and in 1982 participated in an opposition movement publishing political magazines. He was the cofounder of the Democratic Progress Party (DPP) in 1986 and served as secretary general of this main opposition party in Taiwan for three years. He is currently the DPP representative to the United States.

Chu Shulong is a senior fellow in Beijing at the China Institute of Contemporary International Relations as well as a professor at the College of International Relations. He received his Ph.D. in political science from George Washington University in 1993.

Gerrit W. Gong is Freeman Chair and director of the Asia program at the Center for Strategic and International Studies in Washington, D.C. A Rhodes Scholar, he earned his M.A. and Ph.D. in international relations from Oxford University and has served on the research faculties of Oxford, Johns Hopkins, and Georgetown Universities. Gong's U.S. government positions include special assistant to two ambassadors at the U.S. embassy in Beijing and special assistant to the under secretary of state for political affairs.

Harry Harding is dean of the Elliot School of International Affairs at George Washington University. He has been on the faculties of Swarthmore College and Stanford University. He has also been a senior fellow in the Foreign Policy Studies Program at the Brookings Institution. He received his M.A. and Ph.D. in political science from Stanford University.

A professor of economics at Brandeis University, Gary H. Jefferson has concentrated his interests on development, transition economics, industrial organization, and China. He received M.A.s from the Fletcher School of Law and Diplomacy and the London School of Economics and a Ph.D. from Yale University. In the 1986–1987 academic year, he was a Fulbright Scholar at Wuhan University in China.

Loh I-cheng moved to Taiwan in 1948 where he served as an interpreter and interrogator for United Nations forces during the Korean War, for which he received the Medal of Freedom from the U.S. government. In 1979 he was appointed ROC ambassador to Guatemala and was ambassador to South Africa from 1990 to 1997. A former journalist, he contributes to the *United Daily News* and the *China Times*, two of Taiwan's leading newspapers.

Born in 1943, Tao Wenzhao is a research professor and deputy director of the Institute of American Studies at the Chinese Academy of Social Sciences (CASS). Wenzhao was a government-sponsored visiting scholar at Georgetown University from 1982 to 1984 and K.C. Wang fellow of the British Academy in 1993. He is now leading a study on current Sino-U.S. relations, which is one of the key projects of CASS.

Nancy Bernkop... ...Jni-
versity. She is a... ...East
Asian relations,... ...and
Hong Kong. He... ...1 to
serving in differ... ...1e is
a frequent guest... ...ine,
Fox in Depth, an...

Born in 1960, W... ...the
University of Zh... ...s an
associate researc... ...Chi-
nese Academy o... ...pa-
pers published t...

An assistant pro... ...van
University, Phili... ...Na-
tional Taiwan U... ...7 of
Virginia. His ex... ...the
University of To... ...has
been awarded a... ...ica-
tion Fellowship. ...g>.

Born in Shangh... ...hai
University of In... ...985
he joined Shangh... ...as-
sistant. Beginning in 1991, he studied at the School of Advanced International Studies at Johns Hopkins University, where he received his M.A. in international public policy. Gancheng's focus is on U.S.-China-Taiwan relations.